D0938746

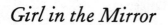

*Girl in the Mirror*

Also by Natasha Tarpley

*Testimony*
*I Love My Hair* (children's book)

NATASHA TARPLEY

# Girl in the Mirror

## THREE GENERATIONS
## OF BLACK WOMEN
## IN MOTION

Beacon Press

Boston

Beacon Press
25 Beacon Street
Boston, Massachusetts 02108-2892
www.beacon.org

Beacon Press books are published under the auspices of
the Unitarian Universalist Association of Congregations.

03 02 01 00 99 98       8 7 6 5 4 3 2 1

This book is printed on recycled acid-free paper that contains at least
20 percent postconsumer waste and meets the uncoated paper ANSI/NISO
specifications for permanence as revised in 1992.

Text design by Christopher Kuntze
Composition by Wilsted & Taylor Publishing Services

Library of Congress Cataloging-in-Publication Data

Tarpley, Natasha.
Girl in the mirror : three generations of black women in motion /
Natasha Tarpley.
p.   cm.
ISBN 0-8070-7202-8 (cloth)
1. Afro-Americans—Fiction.   I. Title.
PS3570.A6474G57   1998
813'.54—dc21                                  97-43289

*To Marlene & Anna Mae,*
*wings*

*i am not done yet*

as possible as yeast
as imminent as bread
a collection of safe habits
a collection of cares
less certain than i seem
more certain than i was
a changed changer
i continue to continue
where i have been
most of my lives is
where i'm going

—LUCILLE CLIFTON

*Some say our story begins in the middle of an ocean, in the belly of a monster, at the mercy of demons. Others say that we began with a hammer and a nail; that we laid our bodies down and raised cities along our spines. But I say it goes deeper than that, deeper than cotton fields and human cargoes, the thick and heavy links of a history we're constantly trying to break, to desire. The urge that stirs you in the middle of the night, grabs you by the spine and jerks your head upright. The story begins here, when we realize that we are no longer asleep, and the beat of our hearts sounds just like the beat of a faraway drum. And it is at this moment of unrest, when our hearts refuse to allow us to be still, that we realize what we must do, which is to gather ourselves up and move.*

# I

# ANNA

*Movement and Rest*

# Anna 1942

Dear Jack,

So there it was. The emptiness he left behind had beat me back to the house and was already in the kitchen, leaning back in Jack's chair and grinning with its feet propped up on the table. Don't look as you pass, just keep walking to the stove, eyes steeled on the coffeepot. Light the burner beneath the kettle. Reach for two cups hanging on the hook above the sink. Remember. Take down one. There's a clean saucer in the dish drain. Doesn't match your cup. Use it anyway. Stand on tiptoe to reach the coffee tin in the cabinet over the stove. Jack was supposed to finish that footstool before he left. Maybe you can ask one of the brothers. Maybe Buddy or Herb'll do it. Four tablespoons of coffee for the percolator. Too much. Three teaspoons of sugar in the cup. No, that's what Jack takes. Jack always did have a sweet tooth. Steady yourself against the stove. Get it together, girl. Get yourself together. Leave that cup and start over. One tablespoon coffee, one teaspoon sugar. That's your cup. Already the kettle is singing and you haven't even got the cream out the box. Usually you end and the kettle begins on the same note. You slipping girl. Get it together. Get yourself together.

*All of us here are doing fine.*

Somehow when I turned around, I half-expected the emptiness to be gone. Chased away by the clatter of cups and saucers, the rattle of coffee grounds, the spoon clinking against the side of my cup as I stirred and kept stirring until I could get up the nerve to turn around. The emptiness was still there. And now that I was facing it, the only thing left to do was to go on over to the table and sit down.

"Mornin'," said the emptiness. I didn't say anything.

"Aw, come on, Anna. Don't be that way. I didn't do nothin' to you for you to be acting so mean. Can I at least have a smile this mornin'? Just one itty bitty smile?" I kept my eyes on my coffee.

"You know, sooner or later you gonna have to make peace with me."

I sat upright and opened my mouth but no sound came out.

"What you gonna say, gal? Wasn't nothin' you could say to keep that man here, and ain't nothin' you can say now that he gone. Face it. Me and you gonna be like two peas in this little house. That's all there is to it."

And sure enough, when I went to make the bed, the emptiness was there in the sheets still wrinkled in the shape of his body. It was there, pressed up against me as I cleaned the greens for supper, breathing down my neck and begging for a taste when I bent to check the ham browning in the oven. It was stretched back in the armchair as I dusted around the living room, rippling through the dirty water left over from the wash, swaying with the clothes blowing like ghosts on the line.

*How was your ride? I hope I packed enough for you to eat.*

I had to get out. Go somewhere away from the house where I could feel the heat prickling on my skin, and where there was air that wasn't already heavy with Jack's scent. Down the road, about a quarter mile, Jack's parents were working in the yard outside their house. The brothers would be out in the field rising over the horizon behind the house. Their wives and Jack's sisters would be home, cooking their part of the family dinner we would all get together and eat at Mom and Dad's later in the afternoon. All of the kids in Jack's family stayed on their parents' land. As soon as they were ready for a place of their own, or when they got married, Jack's parents would build them a house.

There was always someone within hollering distance, so there were places I could go. But I didn't feel like seeing anybody from the family just yet. And I couldn't go anywhere else because the food was almost done. I made myself content with a glass of iced tea and went out to the side porch which Jack had just finished screening in before he left. I had a chair out there in a dark corner where I liked to sit when I wanted to be alone with my thoughts. I could disappear in that corner, which is exactly what I needed to do.

It wasn't long after I got myself settled and comfortable that Iona Jackson, my friend from down the road, came strolling up the walkway. I never was so glad to see her. I figured with her here I could at least put off the emptiness for awhile, get myself a little peace. Iona would ask what I was doing out in this heat, what smelled so good on the stove. And I would devote myself to answering. I would ask her about the quilting pattern she promised to bring, and did she remember how to do it by heart? And what was it she told me to try adding to my sweet potatoes? Orange rind? Lemon juice? Yes, I would stretch out the small details and string them together, a rope, a trap to harness the emptiness. I cracked an ice cube between my teeth anticipating the conversation, anxious for the company.

But Iona didn't even stop on the porch. She kept on into the house, waving for me to follow.

"Girl, it's too hot to be sitting out there." She sat down at the kitchen table and wiped her forehead with her palm. Iona, too, knew the emptiness and sniffed it out right away, turning up her nose and sucking her teeth at the familiar stench.

"He gone?" she asked.

"Yeah. Left this morning."

"Mmph," Iona snorted. "You be okay." For her the emptiness was a bitter taste on the tongue; the death smell that hovered over the sick and wounded, wafting up from a dark place in her heart. Her hus-

band, Elijah, had gone up North, scattering promises
to write and to send for Iona like rose petals in his
wake. No one had heard from him since. That man
had wound Iona around his finger and just let her
loose, like a pebble in some young boy's slingshot.

But for me, the emptiness was still just a space I
was trying to figure out how to fill, like the scratchy
silence at the end of a record, a kind of music unto
itself that you listen to until you can decide what
you're going to put on next. And maybe I should've
been feeling different from how I was feeling. Maybe
I should've been crying until I didn't have any tears
left or cursing Jack for leaving. But I didn't feel anything but in between, suspended.

I watched Iona drain the glass of tea I had set before her. She stood up and smoothed down her skirt.
I got up, too, and started wrapping the ham cooling
on top the stove.

"Well, I s'pose one of the brothers will be by after
awhile to carry this food down to Mom and Dad's.
You know how Jack's parents eat at four on the dot.
You welcome to join us," I offered, not ready to relin-
quish her company.

"No thanks, sweetheart. I put a pot a beans on earlier and left them simmering. They should be ready
by now. I'll be by tomorrow to check on you."

"At least take some greens," I said rummaging for
a bowl.

"Save 'em for lunch tomorrow," Iona said at the
door. I nodded.

"You take care a yourself, honey, your Jack is fine.
You'll hear from him soon."

I wanted to say that I wasn't worried about Jack,

that I knew he'd call or write when he got settled, but the words wouldn't come. Instead, I waved my hand in front of my face, swatting away what Iona had said.

"I'll see you tomorrow," was all my tongue could grab, as I waved at her all the way down the walkway, and kept on waving after she had closed the front gate behind her and started down the road, even after she had stopped looking back.

*Everything here is the same as you left it. Don't worry about me. I'll be alright until we can be together again in Chicago . . .*

It wasn't until after dinner, as the night started closing in on the sun, like a finger pressed soft against lips, shutting out light like sound, that I began to really notice his absence. And when I was alone in the dark of our bedroom, this was when I started to feel again. The hurt came alive.

I talk to the air, Jack, because that's all of you I've got left. That's all that you left. All your shirts are gone. Ella came by here wanting to borrow a clean one for Buddy to wear to dinner, but the drawer was empty. Nothing but the newspaper lining and a few mothballs rolling around. Seeing that, more than anything, Jack, made me mad. Not because I think you're planning to desert me like Elijah did Iona. I know you're a better man than that. But I'm mad, Jack, because you took the comfort of our house, my grits and eggs warming your belly, our last night together, when we couldn't stop touching and kissing, and I was so soft for you; you took all these things for your strength, packed them away in that big trunk.

You got up this morning, loaded the trunk onto Jackson's old rusty truck, and rode away.

Did you ever stop to listen to my heartbeat, Jack? I would've gotten up with you, traveled all those hours in that truck. I would've lived in one room and found some place to work in Chicago if I had to. Whatever we had, Jack, would've been enough. But you didn't hear me. You couldn't see all that in me. You took everything for yourself. And wasn't nothing left for me but the scraps, bones I got to find a way of piecing back together.

*Everyone misses you and we wish you well. You are in our prayers.*

*Your loving wife,*

*Anna*

# Jack 1942

Night is a curtain drawing back its heavy, sleepy-eyed veil for us to enter its darkest part. You should see how Jackson has his truck rigged up for this trip. He's nailed some flat boards along either side wall like benches, and right before we left Alabama he picked up a nice, sturdy piece of canvas from the hardware store. We all helped him pitch it up over the hatch. We out here looking like a band of outlaws in a covered wagon, or Indians in a roving teepee, but at least there's something over our heads.

Jackson say this is his new business, carrying folks out of Alabama to Chicago. I guess with eight men paying fourteen dollars a piece for the ride and gas, and him making two, three trips a month, he'll make himself a nice piece of money. But then Jackson always could find some way to make a dollar, with his slippery self. Remember how he charged us for the hay ride at the church picnic? Or the time he drove down to New Orleans and came back with all those hoodoo potions, then set up that stand in the back of the truck to sell them? Jack could've been selling swamp water for all we knew, but folks sure lined up. Had their money out even before they got to the table. Yes, Lord. That's one man'll never starve.

Maybe if I had stayed, I could've gotten into something like that, carrying folks up North. Seem like so many want to go these days. Jackson can't handle all those folks by himself. Daddy has that old truck sitting out in the garage. It needs work, but me and Buddy could've probably fixed it up. You know how much my little brother likes to work with his hands. He can fix anything with a motor. But no use bringing it up now, I'm already on my way. Alabama is a cloud of dust rising from beneath the tires. Road already traveled. A fine-grain memory settling in our wake.

Ride's been smooth so far. No trouble. Except for when we pulled out of Warrior, this car full of white boys, kids really, trailed us for about ten, fifteen miles, hollering out the window, nigger this, nigger that. Damn, these folks just don't want to let us go. And it isn't even *us* really. It's the idea of us. The shadow of us. The way they feel like we're always empty and waiting for them to fill us up. Like that dented pail hanging in the pantry that's held everything: rainwater, piss, milk, bleach, dirt, soapy water. Whatever you want to load in that bucket, it'll carry. That's what we've been all this time. I'm not saying that's all we've been, but that's how they look at us.

Shit. I don't want to talk about them anymore. I don't want to talk about us anymore. I want to talk about the air out here. I don't know what makes it so different from the air anyplace else, but, Anna, I swear it runs through me like water, just as cool and clear. Yet there's something heavy to it, stale even. It's the musty smell spilling out from between the pages of those old books your grandmother keeps in her parlor, or the scent of mothballs escaping like a sigh from Mama and Daddy's closet. And still it's more than this. There's something in this air that I can't name.

You remember that time in New Orleans, right before we got married? I had come from Alabama to help your daddy with his harvest from the orchard, and one morning, before we went out, your mama fixed us some biscuits with this red meat gravy for breakfast. You know how much I always enjoy your mama's cooking, but this was something else. That gravy left this feeling in me, like I knew I had eaten it before, but couldn't remember when or where. Soon as I got back to Alabama, I asked Mama if she had ever fixed gravy that way. And Anna, you know what she told me? She said that she never made it herself, but M'Dear, my grandmother, used to make it and mash the biscuits in it and feed it to us when we were babies just starting to teethe.

That's how this air feels to me right now. Like something long forgotten, teetering on the brink of remembrance. But wherever it comes from, whenever I breathed it before, it is doing wonders for all of us right here, right now. Cleaning us out. Folks keep getting up to spit out of the back of the truck. It's the South coming up. All the stuff we kept inside, that dried and crusted on our ribs, hardened around our joints and muscles. The air is moving through my body. No blocked passages. Sinuses clear. Nothing weighing down my chest. No medicine you can buy can give you this feeling. Anna, I wish you could know this freedom.

Nothing to do out here but talk and sleep. I'm lucky I got my flashlight, or else I wouldn't have been able to see to write, though I'm sure my heart would've guided my hand across the page without it (smile). One of the men on the truck knows how to sing any song you can think of. The music is like candlelight, giving us a moment of brightness, a glimpse back into the lives now falling away with the miles.

People like us, who've been in one place all our lives, we get accustomed to things. Like the sky hovering over our heads and homes. We come to think of it as *the* sky. And how we can walk every inch of our land or from one end of town to the other with our eyes closed, or clock the distance between our house and the next town, even the next state over by heart. Then we pack our picnics for the roadside and call ourselves traveling.

But out here, you begin to understand that your sky is just a little thumbnail piece of sky. You begin to understand that no matter where you stop, the roads just keep going on and going on. Anna, the largeness of the world makes me feel so small; as though the wind could pluck me up and blow me away, just one more particle riding this ancient air. What anchors me here?

Above us, the moon shimmers white as a store-bought egg against this night. We toss up the loudness of our voices and dreams like a gigantic stone trying to crack it, to anoint ourselves in its yolk of possibility. The knowledge that the moon can't be broken ignites the talk, makes a man stand up and pace the three steps from the front of the truck to the back, pounding his fist in his palm, spewing out his plans. But it is the idea that it can that makes him settle down in a corner and sift through the ashes of his thoughts, asking himself how he can make it work.

It is the idea that saves us; keeps us hanging together, leaning on one another, here in the darkness. The idea that we all have destiny locked up in our suitcases or stuffed deep in our back pockets, hidden in our socks, strapped around our waists. The idea that our hands can build a new life, can carve

for ourselves and our families a small space out of this vast-
ness.

Some of the men on this truck, I grew up with and know
as well as my name. Some of them have traveled from Bir-
mingham and other towns and states just to make this ride.
There're some out here dressed in plain clothes, and some
out here bleeding, as they say, dressed sharp enough for their
own funeral. Maybe it is a funeral of sorts, because some of us
are dead now to the South, and the South is dead in us; the
turn of a key in the ignition enough to cut ties to the land, to
family. But I am one of those stroking around the navel, feeling the long cord that keeps us connected to home. My heart
is the softness in me, the place where roots have grown deep.
I am one of those who still remembers.

But any way we've come, we're here now, standing at the
edge of this night, black as a spit-cleaned slate. Our reflections, shimmering on its surface, beckon, *Come on, why don't
you? Just jump in.*

# Iona 1942

Moonlight has a way of drawing things out. Things you're trying to hide from other people, things you're trying to hide from yourself. Things you stick way back in the drawer, like your last-resort panties or the stockings with the holes in them, or the linen at the bottom of the pile with the embarrassing stain. These things no one wants to admit that they have, or worse, that they have need for. Because eventually you run out of your best things and you have to turn to your worst. Moonlight goes straight to that secret place and opens it up, all of its contents shining bright on your face.

"Elijah had the prettiest hands I ever saw on a man," I say, leaning back in my chair. Anna and I had been out in the garden, picking collards by moonlight. After washing the greens in the sink inside, we came out here to the side porch to pick off the stems. But an hour had passed and there were still only a few stems and bad leaves collected on the newspaper spread at our feet. Mostly we were out here for the air just starting to turn cool in the evening, to listen to the night sounds—crickets and wind, music drifting down from Buddy's place:

> If you don't have somebody to love you, you don't
> have a doggone thing . . .

I sigh deep in the moonlight, looking past the still-full bowl of collards on my lap, past the fields rippling like water and past the wall of night sky; looking into the black behind my eyes, walking the slow walk toward a pale light of memory that's been burning for me, waiting all these years for my return.

"The prettiest hands," I say. "Elijah say they used to tease him all the time about them. Say he got hands like a girl. Probably 'cause of how much he fussed over them. Every time you looked up that man was trimming or filing or soaking something. Nails look better than mine.

But they were definitely a man's hands, no two ways about it. His fingers were long and slender, with a nice full nail cut even at the tip. Not like those nubs most men got at the ends of their fingers. And his skin, the color of peanut brittle, was pulled tight and smooth so that you could see the bone and the strength rippling whenever he reached out or held something. Oh, I knew those hands. They were the first thing I noticed about Elijah when we met.

You remember when they used to have those dances down at the old Colored Masons' Hall, the one they just tore down year before last? No, you wouldn't remember, Anna, you was still in Louisiana then. That was before you married Jack.

Anyway, they used to have these dances down there, one Saturday a month. Come to think, it might've been sponsored by the church. And honey, that was our big night! Folks would spend the whole week just getting ready. Those Saturday nights, everyone turned out, shoes shined, hair curled, new suits, new dresses. Those colored folks knew they was sharp! But it wasn't 'til the summer after I came out of high school that Mama and Daddy allowed me to go to the dances. I would always watch them get ready and see all the other couples walking by our house—we lived right at the edge of town. That's how I knew what it would be like. But girl, when my time came to go, when me and my girlfriends walked into the hall, it was even better than I imagined.

They had the place decorated so nice, Anna, I wish you could've seen it. They had balloons, Spanish moss, and those crêpe paper streamers hanging from everywhere. There was even a small red carpet laid out at the entrance. Mama had let me borrow one of her dresses, and I was trying to show off my little shape and at the same time walk in the heels she gave me to match the dress. My friends just about had to drag me away from the mirror at the house, but by the time I got to the hall and saw how good everybody else looked, I was ready to turn right back around. So then they had to drag me into the place. I was so timid, Anna. But somehow I managed to lift my eyes enough to make my way over to the punch bowl, and when I had my cup I headed straight for the wallflowers clumped in a corner at the back of the hall.

Every so often, one of my girlfriends would come over and drag me out on the dance floor. And then there was Mama, with her busy self, trying to get me to dance with Robert Griffin, the preacher's son. That's who she had picked out for her son-in-law. But I ended up right back in that corner, and there was always a chair or an empty spot on the wall waiting for me. I didn't have that ease, you know, like my girlfriends. They knew what they wanted from men; knew how to get their attention and talk to them real sweet and nice, so by the time they was finished with them, those boys was hooked and hanging around their fingers.

I knew what kind of man I wanted. In fact, I had this whole collection of fantasies about how we would meet at the supper after church, or in the store, or at one of these dances. He would see me and I would see him. Then we would look at each other, 'til he got up the nerve to speak. And then we would discover how much we had in common. He would be a serious kind of man, and he would see in me a woman who was just as serious as he.

And you know, he would be fine as anything. Tall, smooth chocolate brown, cute little behind and gentle, real soft-spoken. Oh, honey! I wanted a man who knew what to do when the lights went out and then could turn around and debate Mr. Du-bois and Booker T.! He would know all these parts of me and how to satisfy them, see. Really do sound like a fantasy, huh? But I was young and stubborn. I was determined that I was going to get this man. *But* I wanted him to find me. I wanted him to notice my eyes or my smile or my new dress. He would find the beauty in me. I didn't want to have throw it up in his face.

The problem with waiting, though, is that the person you waiting on may never come. By the time I got to that dance, I was beginning to think that this was the case. And I was mad. Doesn't make sense, being mad at somebody you don't even know. But I started carrying that anger, like this cushion around my heart, although I still had hope for that man. I could still see him when I closed my eyes at night. But instead of going out there and looking for him, I decided to take what came. And what came generally wasn't worth nothing. So I started to think to myself, maybe that's all I can get; maybe that's all I'm worth.

Then here come Elijah, strutting down that line of hopeful women crossing they fingers that he stop at them. But he came straight to me, girl. He picked me out of all them

women. One of them gals looked something like Lena
Horne, too, had that pretty hair, nice yellow complexion. But
he didn't stop at her, slowed down, but didn't stop. He came
to me. And while he was standing in front of me, I just kept
staring at his hands, you know. I had never seen such pretty
hands on a man. I took a quick peek at the rest of him, but,
really, the hands was enough for me.

He asked me to dance, and I said, yes. All the while I'm
thinking, What he want with me? What could this fine man
with beautiful hands want with me? That's what kept spinning over and over in my head. Even after we were seeing
each other regularly, I would look at those hands and count
myself lucky.

Things started out good. He would come by the house and
sit and talk with Daddy, help him out around the farm. I was
proud of him. He took care of himself, dressed well, treated
me nice. On Saturdays, he would take me into town for ice
cream, and we would sit and talk about what was going on in
the world.

I thought he was smart, had opinions. But soon, I came to
realize that Elijah was what I call a 'headline man.' You know,
somebody go through all the headlines in the paper that week
and know a little something about the important stories. But
you ask him about something that hadn't been in the news, or
want to go further into a topic than they had in the paper, the
man was at a loss. Now, I've always been one to read and want
to use my mind. I don't have time to sit up and listen to some
fool just spouting off something somebody else said. Tell me
something that comes from your own mind. Why sit up and
waste what God gave you?

With Elijah, though, it was different. I told myself, at least
he's reading the paper. At least he's keeping up with the
world. A whole lot of people don't even do that. Look at all

these folks out here don't even know how to read. I told my-self these things, because I could see my hope unfolding in his hands. No, he wasn't the man I saw when I closed my eyes, but gradually I began to make room in that dream for him. And soon enough, he had pushed that other fellow aside en-tirely.

Mama never did like him, though. Even when he'd come by the house with some fresh flowers for her, a cigar for Daddy, her heart was still hard against him. She'd say, What I need with flowers? I got flowers in the yard right outside my door. Naw, Mama never liked him. Say he too slick for his own good. She told me, Anna, she say, That boy headed straight for the coal mines. And ain't nothin' wrong with a decent man working in the mines, 'cause he can see the dia-mond sparkling through all the tons of soot and rock. He figure he never gonna reach it hisself, but the least he can do is clear away some of the mess to make the dig for his kids a little easier. But Elijah, he don't see nothing but the now. He don't have a dream bigger than his thumbnail. She told me if I married Elijah he would break me open like rock, and if he didn't find anything of use to him inside he would toss me away, move on to the next fool in his path.

But I didn't listen to her, Anna. I thought it was just Mama talking, you know how mothers talk. Besides, I knew I was strong enough to take care of myself, and him, too, if he needed me. I couldn't get that picture out of my mind of him walking toward me that night, his hands reaching for me, still amazed that it was me he wanted. It shouldn't have been enough, but it was. I wanted to be in love, wanted to be mar-ried, had wanted that since before I started high school. So, I went ahead and married him.

Daddy talked to the white man in town sold us our land and got us a deal on this nice little house not too far from

Mama and Daddy. Elijah didn't have a job when we were married. Didn't have one six months after that or six months after that. He would start something then say it didn't agree with him and go on to something else.

I just kept looking at those hands and seeing how pretty they was and all they could do if given a chance. I thought I could be the one to give it to him. I was cooking for this older white lady in town and taking in wash and ironing on the side. I would get up in the morning before the sun was up, then come home when the sun was on its way down to finish our supper and do my washing. I stopped doing my reading and my studying. Mama had hopes of me going to Tuskeegee to get my teaching certificate, but I let that go, too.

Anna, it got to where I couldn't see the sun rise but through his hands. But I told myself, You got something you wanted, now you got to give something up. You can't have everything. That's what I was telling myself, Anna, sitting up all night waiting for Elijah to come through the door. You can't have everything.

It wasn't until after Mama passed that I began to see I had nothing. I broke my Mama's heart over that man and still had nothing. All those flowers were long since dead, the cigars smoked up, all the sweet things devoured and turning sour in my belly. I had stripped my hands down to the bone, until it felt like there was no more work left in them, nothing more they could do. But even after I realized this, I was still too scared to leave, although I sure as hell stopped giving that nigger my money.

And when the money stopped coming, he started getting restless, sometimes didn't even bother to come home. That's when he started talking about going North.

They got all kinds a jobs up North, in Chicago. Figure it's worth looking into, he say, like he was trying to convince me.

Finally, one night after supper he said, Iona, I got to do right by you. I'ma go on up North and find me a good job. I'ma send for you, too. I'ma make us a good life. I sat there listening to his talk and grinning, because even then I wanted to believe him. But I knew once he was out the door he was gone. And girl, from that time, up to the time he left, that man was so sweet. Guess he figured if he acted nice before he left, that'll spare him from feeling guilty about it when he gone. I sucked up all that sweetness, too. After what I been through, I deserved that little bit.

Sure enough, the morning he left he didn't even wake me to say goodbye. I thought I would be relieved, Anna. I thought I could just pick up my life and keep going. But I was so ashamed of myself, I just curled myself up into a little ball and didn't open up for nobody. I'm ashamed even now to tell about it. I never thought I was the kind of woman just give her life away to the first man who held out his hand. I never wanted to be that kind of woman."

"We all kinds of women, Iona," Anna says.

"All this time gone and I'm just now learning that."

Moonlight raises years of tears, the fresh breath of seasons changing wipes them dry. Pole beans snake over the fence, and the collards wave, *let them go, let them go,* learning how to dance in their wake.

# Anna 1943

I stand tonight on the threshold
    Of a strange mysterious door
That silently opens from the year
    Just gone
To the one that lies before.

The noiseless swing of the hinges
    Is unheard by mortal ear,
But the lurking soul hears the
    Master's voice
Bidding us enter here.

I see not a step before me,
    And I would not if I could,
For I know that to those whom
    Jesus loves
There can happen only good.

Then perhaps the year before me,
    This new way, yet untrod,
May bring my soul to the City
    of Peace
Whose Builder and maker is
    God.

So the door that appeared so forbidding
    That stood like a wall in my way,
Wears a glory bright, when seen
    in the light
Of gate to endless day.

—UNKNOWN

(from the *Christian Recorder*, July 11, 1901)

If you ask her about those days, my mother will tell the story of how her grandmother, nine months pregnant, got on a boat propelled by moonlight that carried her many nights across the water. Nobody knows where the boat was coming from. All we know is that it got to New Orleans, and Mama's mama, my grandmother, was born on the day of the Emancipation Proclamation, out of the clenched fist of slavery, and cradled in the palm of freedom.

This freedom, before the cradle turned into a forest of fingers tangled up and twisted back, one around the other, is what Mama kept wrapped in a little bundle beneath her tongue, tied up with a silk ribbon in the box of papers on top the wardrobe. That first breath of relief, lungs opening wide as sky, milk for the babies they would keep, dreams that still had sweetness, this is what she saved for us. And if you ask her about those days, maybe she will wonder whether these things were enough. But her lips will be drawn into thin, bloodless lines across her face; lines already crossed in a boat drawn by moonlight; lines that mark the beginning of memory.

My daddy's mother was a free woman born of free people, and his daddy was the son of a man whose father had once been master of a plantation. They were in love, so the white man gave Daddy his name, the same name as his white children. Daddy says he grew up with those other kids, his white half-brothers and sisters, and for the longest there weren't any distinctions made between them. Daddy's father built Daddy and his mama a place on his property and stayed up there to their house three nights out of the week. By that time, the white children were grown enough to know the difference between them and Daddy, and grown enough to know where their father was going the nights he kissed them goodnight after supper and walked out the front door.

So there started to grow this bitterness between Daddy and his half-sisters and brothers, until the brothers got together and decided they were going to kill Daddy, or at least run him and his mother off. Every time they'd catch Daddy by himself, they'd beat him. Two or three of them against one man. Finally it got so bad, Daddy had to go and tell his father what was going on. Daddy said the man heard him out and then closed his eyes. When he opened them again they had turned to glass, shiny marbles with a dead blue center. Daddy knew then that in the flicker of that moment, behind eyelids shut like pale pink curtains, his white father had made a choice, had retraced his steps, walking backwards from their little house to his big house, sweeping his footprints off the path, and locked himself behind his heavy front door.

My daddy and his mama left that place after that, as if they had never known it, and settled down right outside New Orleans, with one of his mama's cousins. Daddy decided that he would no longer carry his father's name and peeled it off like work clothes in summer, all used up and smelling. He took his mama's name instead, planted it and watched it grow up from the ground. I remember him all the time telling my brothers, "Put your name on something in this world." That was my daddy's way.

I didn't always have these stories; well, I knew them, but growing up, me and my sisters and brothers, we didn't pay them any attention. They were just snatches of grown folks' talk that you caught here and there. Nobody sat you down and said, listen to this, this is important. These were things we didn't talk about in our family. You learned by watching what your parents did, and you saw the kind of life they tried to give you.

But when you're young, you get hungry for your own taste of life. You start to see all the things you don't have, and all that you want. Then you look at what your parents gave you and feel that it's not enough to satisfy your hunger. You make the choice to leave your parents' house in search of your own version of freedom. My brothers joined the service and went to war. My sister, Rowena, the oldest, married a jazz player and became a nomad on the chitlin' circuit. And Agnes, the next oldest girl, was a wind rushing through our house, but everywhere she turned there was a wall boxing her in, a baby crying that she had to pick up when Mama and Daddy were out in the field. Louisiana was thick with heat and routine that slowed her down, kept her feeling stuck in one place. As soon as Agnes turned sixteen, she packed her bags and breezed out the front door to "get free," in Chicago.

There was a man used to come by our house sometime, a friend of Daddy's mama from those long ago days, the only one would talk about those times. He'd say, "If you was livin'

with the one you love, then you had a taste of freedom. That's
the best you hope for, that's the best there was."

I had my first taste when I married Jack. Oh, I remember
him then. Dark brown with a flush of red rising from beneath
the surface of his skin like something was burning inside of
him; high Cherokee cheekbones he got from his grandmother; waves from out the pomade jar. And I remember myself, an almond-colored beauty and curious, wavering on the
brink of my parents' dreams.

Jack came knocking at our door one day. I don't know who
it was answered, but whatever he said got him inside. Me and
my younger sister, Leona, ran to see who it was. Jack was
standing there in the front room talking to Papa, looking
humble—everyone looked humble in front of Papa—but determined. I heard him telling Papa how he was from Warrior,
a small town in Alabama where his people owned a nice-sized
farm and dairy. He was in Louisiana for a few weeks taking
pictures and selling portraits door to door. He wanted to
open his own photographer's studio back home and was here
trying to get the money to cover his first month's rent and
expenses. He must've been twenty at the time—I was sixteen—and still a little rough around the edges. But even
then, he acted like an old man, so serious, his forehead already creased into chicken feet from the way he frowned up
his face when he was concentrating hard on something,
which was nearly all the time.

I noticed how he talked to my daddy, holding his eye for
every word he said. And I noticed how Daddy listened to
him, with his arms folded across his chest, his head slightly
tilted to the left. The same way he listened to Mr. Fontaine,
the white man who sold him his seed, or Mr. Herrell, who
owned the colored grocery and bought Daddy's fruit and
vegetables for his store.

I don't know if we really could afford a family portrait at

the time, but I knew Mama and Daddy wanted to. And Daddy was impressed with Jack, especially the fact that he came from good people like us, who worked hard and owned their property. I couldn't tell who was more pleased, Jack or Daddy, when Mama brought back the money I had heard her counting out from the coffee can they kept hidden in the pantry and pressed it into Jack's palm.

He took the money like a gentleman, waiting until Mama offered before he stretched out and opened his hand. He closed his fingers around it without looking down, slipped the coins noiselessly into his pocket, and then shook Mama's and Daddy's hands. We sat for the picture the following afternoon, and Jack delivered it to us a week later. Daddy was so taken with him, he invited Jack back that fall to help him in the orchards during picking season. And Jack came, and kept coming, each season, taking back to Alabama a bag of our fruit and more and more of my family's heart.

Mama and Daddy had just started letting me and Leona entertain young men at the house, so we were used to boys appearing on our doorstep, the air around them flooded with the scent of English Leather cologne, foreheads and ears shining with Dixie Peach pomade and sweat. I guess I just counted Jack as one of their number. Every Wednesday evening, the fellows from the Boys Home across the road would start trickling through the door. Daddy would get out his chair and sit up there in the living room with us, keeping his eyes glued to those poor boys. There was one guy who could cook—he did the cooking over at the home—and when he came by, he would stay in the kitchen baking or frying up something for the rest of us to eat. Then there were a couple fellows who could sing and a few who would teach us the latest dances.

But the thing of it was, I could only imagine those boys in

the space of Wednesdays, counting down the hours between six o'clock and nine, when Mama would appear in the doorway of the front room winding her clock.

"Papa, what time you say it was?" she'd ask Daddy. That would send the boys scrambling for their coats, gathering up their records and grease-stained paper bags bulging with leftover food. Those boys losing shine, shedding magic, melting into rivers at our doorstep, receding into darkness.

Jack was the only one who lingered, after the company was gone, in the living room with Daddy or having coffee in the kitchen with Mama. His scent surprised from dusty corners, dangled from the walls. He lingered, at the back door of my dreams, waiting for me to let him in. But to me, Jack was more like a pair of old shoes, comfortable, yes, but nothing you look forward to putting on every day. I was waiting for love that would explode in my heart, crack it open like a pecan and expose all that sweetness inside. Then I would know, this is it, this is the one. But there wasn't any explosion, no BOOM when I thought about Jack. So I ran, tried to get as far away from him as I could. I treated him so badly, poor thing. Wouldn't hardly speak to him after the first season he came back. Soon enough, though, I learned that love that cracks you open doesn't leave you anything but broken. I stopped running and turned to look behind me. Jack was still there waiting.

That next picking season, the third year Jack came walking up the dirt path to our house with his powder blue cardboard grip, shirtsleeves rolled up to his elbows, and dressed in creased brown pants and brown suspenders, I opened the door. Jack entered my heart as easy as a hand slides into a glove, as though there was no place else he belonged.

Mama and Daddy weren't altogether thrilled about me and Jack. Even though they had come to love him as a son, they had a hard time, at first, accepting him as my husband. It was like some people see a picture of some place in a magazine, and they say, I'm going to go to that place, 'cause they like the way the picture looks. Then maybe they go there, and nothing they see looks like the picture. They feel cheated somehow, even though what they found may be better than what they went for. Mama and Daddy were still holding on to the picture they had in their minds of the type of man they wanted for their daughters. Mama wanted me to marry a fair-skinned man, maybe someone Creole like us. Daddy wanted somebody rich.

But I chose Jack, crossed the mountain of my parents' dreams and expectations to get to him. He harvested my love, savored it on his tongue and swallowed it, so that it would grow and continue inside of him, and every year I could watch it blossom on his face.

The morning we left Louisiana the sky was white as canvas. I looked deep into that sky, looked deep into my life, and gathered all my dreams around me: the ones I had about becoming an opera singer, or practicing my sewing until I was good enough to be a seamstress and design my own line of dresses. I took those old things and I folded them up, packed them away in that special room in my heart that Mama told me to always keep for myself. I draped myself in Jack's name, in the happiness born in our hands, the life waiting for us in Warrior in the little house that Jack's parents had built for us on their land.

I was so certain then—about how my life would turn out, about freedom. Freedom was the choice Jack and I had made to be together, the possibility that grew up out of the ground and our parents' sweat. For me, this was enough. But Jack always wanted to have something of his own. Although he loved working on his mama and daddy's farm, he couldn't see it as his. Whenever he talked about the place, it was always,

My daddy's property. Mama's milk wagon. In all those hundreds of acres, he could never find any room for himself. I thought that if I opened myself wide as a field, I could make him see that there was some other room for growing; or if I folded myself into his needs, his curves and his edges, I could satisfy his hunger, quiet his restlessness.

The first year of our marriage was relatively still, as we settled into one another and made our home together. Jack kept working his father's land, digging in the soil as though he was trying to pass right through it. One day, Jack saw his chance bubble up to the surface. He took it and rode it all the way to Chicago.

At first when Jack left, I would come out here on the porch and watch the days drip down off of the sun, the days peeling back like pages, breaking into small pieces, slipping through my fingers. And I would wonder, How did I get here? How did my life turn out like this? You look for signs in your life that tell you to choose this path and not another, or that you're going to wind up here, as opposed to someplace else. You look for the signs and hope they lead you in the right direction. But sometimes even if you get a sign you never know if you're reading it right; it may mean something completely different from what you thought. I know this from my daddy. He could see the future.

Daddy knew things he didn't even know he knew. Like when Mama had the baby, a little girl. She was our sister and she died. Daddy had had this dream long before she was born. In it, he saw a cypress branch, a symbol of mourning, waving above our house. He was in bed right beside Mama, but somehow he could see through the roof up into the sky. He could see the stars and the moon just like he was standing outside. That's where the cypress was, hanging over our house by itself not connected to anything.

At the time, we thought the dream might've been about

my brother, Wilton, who was down with a fever. Mama had come in from the fields one day and found him laid out on the front porch. Wilton was always sickly, pretended to be anyway, because he never wanted to do any work. But this time he was sick for real. Mama hung some swamproot around his neck and wrapped him in leaves to draw out the fever. When she went to change them, the leaves were so dried out from the heat from Wilton's body, they would crumble beneath her fingers. Mama and Daddy were up every night and morning praying for him, and after awhile the fever broke. Daddy didn't have any more cypress dreams.

About a year later, Mama had a baby girl. The baby died without warning, just a few weeks after she had learned to walk. Mama was crushed, seemed like she could have died herself, losing that child. None of us could believe this had happened, especially since the baby hadn't appeared to be sick or weak, nothing like that. Daddy went over his dreams, and he came back to the one about the cypress. It made sense now. The baby dying was what the dream was about. But at that point, it didn't matter. All we could do was keep on living.

I had seen the signs months ago. All those nights Jack got up from the table, hungry for something my hands couldn't make him, the distance between us my body couldn't fill. And then when he finally decided he was going to go . . . I read the signs as telling me I needed to work harder, give more. I put all my cards on the table, only to find out that Jack had kept his best hand in his back pocket. But even then, I wasn't ready to let go of my belief, my hope, that love would be freedom enough for the both of us.

I remember one afternoon in Louisiana, before I married Jack, when Mama and her three sisters were sitting up in the kitchen making the Sunday gumbo and gossiping. Mama let me stay in there with them. I was so proud, because usually Mama didn't tolerate her children sitting up under grown folks. I felt like I was a woman that day. My aunt Mary told a story which Mrs. Henry, her friend down at the church, had told her.

"Henry tell me they found Erlene Labateau sleeping out in her field."

Aunt Emma said, "I don't see how they find her in all that high grass. Place looks like shit. She done let all that land go since Paul died. What she wanna go sleep out there for?"

"They ask her, and she say she waitin' on Paul to come home."

Aunt Bertha clucked her tongue. "Poor thing. Man's been dead now two years and she still cain't accept it."

"Poor thing my ass" Aunt Emma say. "She a damn fool for letting herself get all bent up over some man."

"Tha's right!" Mama said, as she stirred the gumbo, then turned to point her spoon at me. "I don't care how much you call yourself loving somebody, you don't ever let nobody get inside you where they can take your heart and twist and use it up any way they want to, and you sittin' waiting for them to give it back when they finished with it. You hear me? You understand what I'm tellin' you?"

I said yes that day, but after Jack left I often imagined myself as that woman perched in the high grass, holding on to the yearning, if I couldn't hold on to him. I didn't know myself anymore without him, without the patterns and the rituals of our life together.

How does a woman relearn her own geography?

Gradually, after the initial hurt began to wear off, I started seeing less and less of myself in that field; as though I was expanding in all directions, getting too big for all of me to fit in the space I had cleared for myself in my imagination. Finally, I was ready to get up from there entirely and start walking. I walked back through the house, kept on past my memories, until I reached the door to the room which my mother had opened up for me and told me to keep, but which I had forgotten I had. I entered that dusty room and pushed aside the mess of Jack's things, Mama's and Daddy's things, in order to clear a place for myself. I looked for my old dreams and found them mixed in with the clutter. I shook them out and saw that they were still good. I draped myself in old garments and made them new again.

I sat in that room, until beneath the wind I could hear silence, and, beneath the silence, there was my heartbeat. It was new to me, this sound, the forcefulness of it in my chest. But I memorized it, promising myself to always walk in its rhythm, to let this sound be the first thing I listened for in the morning, the last thing I heard before closing my eyes at night. I sat in that room, until I was ready to stand up and walk back into the world. I closed the door and locked it, looked for someplace safe to keep the key, somewhere I could get to it quickly when I needed it, maybe tucked in the spiral of my braids, or, better, wrapped in the valley beneath my tongue.

# Anna 1943

In my dreams I am straight
and smooth, flat as a drum
But beneath my girdle,
I am spreading out from all places
I am fat with pickles and grits and Jack,
who has gone to the factories, North,
where the night swallows him
and where he can't find the stars beneath his
     windowsill
Each day it's harder
to fasten the clasps on my dress,
and the weight of myself gets in the way
I have already lost the rhythm
that kept me tight and regular
Soon I will lose my toes to this swelling,
to this child, eating me alive from the inside out
But I am trying to save all of this, Jack,
to hold myself in until your hands
let loose the roundness of my belly

# Anna 1944

I'm sitting out here on the porch, waiting for my sisters, Rowena and Agnes, to come pick me up. They're driving in from Chicago. We're going to stop and see Mama and Daddy in Louisiana and then we'll be on our way back to the city. That's right, *we*. I've decided to go back with them. I'm moving on, girl, moving on. I wish you had been here, Iona, so I could've said goodbye face to face; maybe we would've carried you on up there with us. You need to get yourself out of here. What you got going for you except a couple of deadbeat niggers who'll run you to an early grave? Alright, I won't start that this early in the morning. Besides, this is to say goodbye to the old and greet the new.

I know you're wondering how I made up my mind to go. It was like this: After Jack left, I had time to think about things. And it wasn't so much thinking as listening. It was like the noise of my life, the rhythms by which I counted my moments and my days, had quieted down or been overtaken by this new sound, and it frightened me. I didn't know what to do with myself.

I would get up and come out here, like always, and watch the sun rise. Then I'd put my breakfast on. You know, it took me the longest time to figure out how to make grits for one. Before, I could judge my portion by Jack, because I knew how much he would eat and then I'd pour a little bit on top of that for me. It was a mess, girl. And even when I got to the point where I could cook for just me and do my little bit of washing and cleaning, all I was really doing was modifying the old routine, making it smaller. I'd end up with stretches of time I didn't know how to fill, waiting for the sun to go down so I could go to bed.

I couldn't surrender my life the way it used to be; couldn't face up to the fact that those old ways had flown out the door with Jack and by now were probably skeletons along the roadside. That's what gave me the hardest time, trying to reconcile how my life could be gone and I'm still here.

We girls grow up watching our mamas, seeing the way they take care of the men in their lives—husbands, brothers, sons. We see them cooking, and making sure the house look nice, and going out in the field, too. Then we see the love that blossoms out of all that work they do. The men treat them good, as far as we know; their families are healthy. And we think to ourselves, I want love like that. So we use what we think we've learned from our mothers, which is how to sacrifice, in order to get a man and a piece of that love. I say what we think we learned, because that's only one part of what they tried to teach us. Mama was always telling me, "Go out there and find somebody who gives you the kind of love you need; never let anybody take advantage of you; don't give everything you got to nobody." All those things I never listened to, because I didn't know how to do or not to do what she was trying to tell me.

When you're in love, you get so carried away over the fact that somebody loves you, somebody wants to marry you. Your heart swells up enough for both you and him, and you want to empty yourself out so you can fill more of yourself up with this love. You hand over your life like it was a piece of sweet potato pie, and you watch him pull the plate close to him, then hold your breath until he takes the first bite and smiles. But then he'll come back for seconds and thirds, and you'll keep dishing it out. And what does that leave you but the crumbs of a life somebody else has devoured? See what I mean? This is what my mama was trying to get me to do, to save some of that goodness for myself.

But I say again, I didn't know how. I only knew how to do what I saw my mama do: fix my daddy's plate night after night and clean up the mess he left behind. I'm just beginning to see how Mama kept her words and pieces of herself in the kitchen with the sharp knives. And, when she had to, she wasn't afraid to use them, or to pull them out just to admire the way they glinted in the light, reflecting her face along the cutting line.

I began to find ways to fill up my days. I went back to my sewing, started listening to my music again. But I still missed Jack; my heart is with him. Then I started to think, Why should he be the one say when we're going to be together and where? I asked myself, What am I sitting up here for, waiting on him to send for me when I'm ready and got a way there? Shoot, maybe there's something I want to see myself in Chicago. That's how it happened, how I came to want to go.

I've been packing all week, and, after all that work, ain't carrying nothing but my clothes, the dishes, and some sheets. When I first decided to go, I was around here for days worrying about how I would send for the furniture, how I could fit everything I wanted to take in the car. I had chairs and lamps, even that end table from the living room stacked up by the door, hoping we'd find a way to tie them up on top of the car.

I used to watch other folks going North and be horrified at how much stuff they left behind. But as this day got closer, I understood a little better, for all those things began to feel like clutter. They lost their meaning. Even the dining room table I died for and the bedroom set Jack bought me on our first anniversary. We think our lives hinge on, are anchored by, the things we collect. But really it's us that gives those things feeling and meaning. That's how you can compress your life into such small spaces—three cardboard suitcases, three boxes, two trunks—and it still can feel just as large.

Jack's mama wants the living room furniture, and Herbert and his new wife are going to take the stuff from the bedroom and the dining room, but you come on over here and help yourself if there's something you want. I told everybody that it was alright, so there shouldn't be any problem.

Looking from the outside, it seems so easy just to pack up, honk your horn, wave to your neighbors along the way, and be gone. The old folks spit into the trail of dust and smoke, "Look at 'em, leaving everything behind. Just gone walk away from the place they was born like it ain't nothin'." But it isn't like that. Nothing easy about this. It's like being at your own funeral some ways; how when you turn and lock the door and walk down the porch steps, it's like putting part of your life in the ground. When my grandmother died, I sat up in the living room where they had the coffin for two days, just looking at her, as though staring at her body kept her there with me. But I couldn't watch them bury her.

It's the finality of the thing that gets me. It's the small voice that still wonders if maybe life could've been saved, other choices made. Maybe I could've made myself happy here, been more patient waiting for Jack, moved back home with my folks in Louisiana. That's why once I close the door, I don't look back at the house. I can't bear to see that part of my life that's still alive in there waving at me from the front window.

Well, Iona, here comes the car pulling into the drive, stirring up a thin veil of dust. Jack's brothers are here to help load everything. I guess some part of me half-expected a more majestic passage; that the car would look like a chariot, as the song says, coming up toward the house. But the car looks just the same as in the pictures they sent me from Chicago, and Agnes and Rowena for sure ain't no angels (smile).

They've pushed all that stuff in the car, Lord only knows how, and there's just enough room for me in the back seat. All my goodbyes have been said. My journey begins with the awkward jolt of shifting gears; the crunch of gravel beneath the tires; no tears, no looking back; a prayer for a smooth ride . . .

# Anna 1944

Watching the evening turn reminds me of peeling back the petals of a rose, the sky blushing in layers of blue to pink to orange to red to purple. Up front, Henry, Rowena's husband, Rowena and Agnes bicker about whether we should pull off the road for a while. Henry keeps his eyes focused straight ahead, his shoulders square.

"This the worst time to stop out here. Driving with Illinois plates. Too much happens to colored people on these roads. There was a lynching around here just a couple months ago."

"But Henry," Rowena half-pleads, half-snaps, "you gone wear yourself out. You already tired as it is. You liable to run us off the road."

"Rowena, as much as we been traveling with the band, having to be at a gig in one town one day, another one the next, you should know better. You the last person should be calling me tired . . ."

"Well, if the shoe fit . . . ," Agnes pipes. Henry tosses her a dismissive look out of the corner of his eye.

"I still say we try to make it to the next big town. I think Jack told me they got a filling station with a colored toilet near the highway," he says to no one in particular.

"Shit, that place liable to be so nasty, you don't even want to squat there," Agnes smirks.

"I'd rather go in the bush myself," Rowena chimes.

"Damn!" Henry slams his hand down on the steering wheel. "Can't you two shut up your complaining for one minute? One minute that's all I want. You all the ones gonna drive us off the road. If I'da known I'd be hauling a load of cackling hens, I never woulda taken this gig. Jesus God!"

"Quit your ranting, Mr. Turner, and just pull off the road. Anybody try something, I'll protect you."

"One more word, Agnes, and I'll pull off alright, just long enough to put you out. You'll be walking to Chicago, gal. I hope you got on some comfortable shoes." Henry, trying to sound mad, but I can tell he's smiling. All of us are now, as the tension from the argument flies out the window into the evening air.

Henry veers slowly off of the two-lane highway—one lane going in each direction—and the car grumbles to a halt on the gravel shoulder near a thick clump of bushes set back from the road.

"Y'all please hurry up now, I got to go too," he says, opening his door to let his legs hang out as he stretches back on the seat. Agnes and Rowena jump out of the car as I unfold myself from my cramped space, lodged in between one of the big trunks and the door.

"How you making out back here?" Rowena asks, her chin jutting over the top of the open door. "If you want, me or Agnes could switch with you."

"I told you when we left Alabama that I'm fine where I am. If I move up front then I'm still gonna be crowded between Henry and one of you, so what's the difference?"

"Okay, okay, stop fussing. I was just trying to make sure you were all right . . . "

"You got the toilet paper?" I ask, fishing around in my bag.

"Yeah, Agnes got some. Come on come on come on . . ." Rowena says, hopping from one leg to the other.

"You all don't sit too close to the ground now," Henry grins. "Some snake's liable to mistake your behind for his dinner and jump up and bite you." He claps his hands together for emphasis.

"Forget you, Henry," Rowena sucks her teeth at him.

"Baby, you wish you could . . ." Henry calls after us.


When we get back to the car, Agnes opens the trunk and lifts out a brown paper shopping bag, heavy with the food Mama had packed for us in Louisiana. I spread a few sheets of yesterday's newspaper on the hood before emptying the bag's contents. There's fried chicken, white bread and pound cake, a plastic container of fruit salad made from the harvest of Daddy's orchard, and two tall thermoses, one filled with lemonade, the other with cold chicory coffee. Rowena hands out the plates, forks, and cups I brought for us to use on the road.

"One thing I can say for the country," Henry says when he returns from the bushes, "they got good air out here." He reaches for the jug on the floor in the front of the car and pours water over his hands, a calm settling over him.


We eat to the sound of crickets and small breezes rustling through the grass. And after the last crumb has been devoured and the wrappings collected, we linger in the stillness of the night. Henry lights a cigar, its burning orange tip piercing the darkness.

"You don't get quiet like this in Chicago," he says, blowing smoke. "Soak it up now, Anna."

I smile. "Anywhere I go, I'll find me a little piece of quiet."

"Well, you ain't been to Chicago," Agnes remarks. "Just ask Rowena."

"That's right . . . Ain't nowhere like Chicago," Rowena agrees. "When I first got there, I couldn't sleep for a month, I was so nervous. Every time you look up somebody honking the horn, screaming out the window . . . Lawd, I was a wreck."

"But I helped you relax, didn't I, babe?" Henry wraps his arms around her from behind and kisses her neck.

"Oh, go on, Henry," Rowena flusters out of his grasp.

"Come on, baby, dance with me." Henry grinds his cigar out in the dirt with the heel of his shoe and takes Rowena in his arms once again. They press together, gravel crunching beneath their feet, Henry singing under his breath.

I look away. Something in me strains. My insides clench with a tightness that begins between my legs and runs the entire length of my body to my teeth. Agnes reaches for me and I allow myself to be lifted from my perch on the front fender. We dance at arm's length, swaying to Henry's singing, as the last whisper of sunlight slips beneath the horizon, the sky turning seamless, a deep black-purple, like the unblemished skin of an eggplant.

Back in the car, I drift into sleep listening to my sisters spinning tales, Henry humming something sweet, the faint smell of cigars wafting through the air. I dream of Jack's smiling face waiting for me, just beyond the horizon.

# Jack 1944

*Ranaway: A Negro named Jack.*

   This same dream. In the haze between asleep and awake, a wavy film rising like heat, I see myself walking. A beam of steel glints in the moonlight, the rusted shoulder of a deserted railroad track. An empty suitcase bangs against my knees. The ghosts of trains cup my ears in a wheeze once whistle. The dream always leads me here, to this inevitable graveyard of desire bounding out of step with time, dreams rattling my pockets like spare change. Memory shutters.

   *A likely fellow, about twenty-six or twenty-seven years of age. Of proud stature and stubborn disposition. Appears taller than he is . . .*

   Remembering . . . feels more like being lifted out of my body and set down at the beginning to walk the distance of my life again and again.
   . . .

Three pairs of hands rest on a table. My father's large hands are stacked one on top the other, fingers pointing in opposite directions. Mother extends her arms, fingers interlocked, palms pressed together as in prayer. My own hands bear down flat, thumbs curled around to grip the table's edge.

The *Chicago Defender* lies open in the center, now a still white flag between us. But it wasn't always. Its pages worn thin, black ink fading to gray, disappearing, could testify to the number of times we sat at the table like this and spread the paper out, running anything with a point—pencils, fingers, ink pens, knives—along the lines of print, poking holes in the crowded promises of advertisements for jobs, the smiling faces of Negroes.

They hadn't wanted me to go from the beginning. I was the only son who truly took an interest or had a talent for the land. My brothers had been seduced by the quickness of steel; had wrapped themselves around triggers and war and returned home shells, potential hardened. Their blank faces, their eyes, all flash and fire, became the mirrors predicting the future of the land in my absence.

"What about when I get old?" my father laments, empty palms turned upward. Hadn't I been the one to get up every morning with the sun? Hadn't I contributed the money I earned selling portraits so that we could buy the last hundred acres? What about my wife? Why leave it all behind?

But the questions have been swept into a pile in a far corner, their place on the table surrendered to the letter, typed on crisp white paper, from my cousin in Chicago, light catching the big words: Opportunity. Adventure. Expecting. Employment. Supervisor. Permission. Confirmed. Nobody touches anything. Daddy gets up from the table and says to me, "You are used to putting your hands in the ground and pulling something up. I only wish that was enough."

*Has a handsome and smooth face, skin breathes red from beneath a dark black hue. Speaks good and proper English with a soft tone*

When would it ever be enough?

I remember a night, drawn back like a curtain, inviting me inside. I followed. The moon made it look so easy. Possibility, a white broken line out of Alabama.

When would it ever be enough?

It wasn't like some folks said; that the city would open like a book, my story waiting for me somewhere inside. Emerging out of the clarity of the night before, the city rises in a huff of black smoke and exhaust threatening to bury me alive. There is that feeling again, of floating, of being drawn by somebody else's strength. My cousin meets me that morning, as soon as I step off the truck, and we drive out to Ford Motors where he works.

"Now, I told the man you coming here straight off the farm, so you used to heavy work. Don't tell him nothing about your people owning their land. Say something 'bout how you got a wife and kids to feed, a sick mama, anything. If he ask you how much schooling you've had, tell him you got through grammar school. Don't say nothin' about Tuskeegee. These crackers up here same as back home. They find out you a college-educated nigger and they'll hire you just to ride your ass."

They give me the job. An apron with my name on it. I pour the mold for aircraft engines. Sometimes it's my father's hands melting in the orange glow of steel setting, as somebody else's engine takes shape; bone splintering as I pare away the excess . . .

When would it ever be enough?

Every now and then I see the men who made the ride with me from Alabama. We talk as though someone is watching us, with much shifting and hesitation. Skin sags, crumpled and faded as the paper bags we carry our lunches in. The smell of blood, tar, dirty water, or gasoline precedes us. Our conversation echoes church: the obligatory fall and rise, answers everyone knows before the questions are asked.

*"What you been up to these days?"*
*"Nothin' man, same old thing. Just working, trying to make it . . . you know."*
*"That's everybody . . . How's your wife? Wasn't you married back home?"*
*"Yeah man, but that ain't last. I told her I'ma send for her soon as I get something pay enough. She say she don't wanna leave, and I say I don't wanna go back there, cain't go back there and live. So we went our separate ways . . ."*
*"My wife just got here a few months ago. She's pregnant, you know. We still trying to make our space together. . . . I don't have but one room . . . she's used to more. . . . We had us a house back in Alabama . . ."*
*"But that's nice you all are together. It'll work out, especially with the baby coming. . . . Say, you remember that night, riding in from Alabama?"*
*"Yeah, best night of my life. So clear and dark . . ."*
*"I made a lot of plans that night. Way I figured it then, I shoulda been opened up that restaurant like I wanted."*
*"Maybe you still can. Hell, you a young man."*
*"Naw, Jack, that dream is dead and buried. Some things you*

*got to let go. . . . I got me a good job now, I don't want to mess it up. This place . . . turned out different . . . not at all what I expected. By the way, where you working now?"*

*"Over at Ford. Then I got a job at a filling station on Cottage Grove on the weekends. They gonna make me Assistant Manager over there. I'm thinking about quitting Ford."*

*"Yeah, man, that's alright. Assistant Manager . . ."*

When would it ever be enough?

I hear the sound of blood pulsing. Eyes strain toward something never seen. This constant hum, the thing in me that says, Jack, keep on looking. Maybe you don't know how this feels, to be in a place where you can't make mind and body agree, where your mind squeezes into crevices, into thoughts your body can't follow through. I'm looking for a way to reconcile the dream and the work. The work that doesn't end with the dream, but with itself.

Remember . . . how the sun was the promise you lived by?

*He is well known about town as a good man. We hear he has got sort of an Indenture with him under the Pretense of being Free.*

What is a good man? Is a good man a man who pays the bills? A man who comes home at night? A man who sits at the head of his table? Where is the boundary between the good man and the man who is me? I'm afraid sometimes that someone will look beyond the largeness of this man's shoes and see the small man quaking inside.

*He is supposed to be lurking about town, as his wife is with child.*

Anna's stomach swells. A moon measuring the tide of my life. An eye that strips me naked, to bone. At times, when I am near her, I feel like there isn't enough room, enough air in the place for the both of us.

I love her. Love that there's somebody waiting for me in that little room when I get off work at night. She's made the place into a home. Started back with her sewing and we have drapes now hanging in the window. She made a nice quilt for the bed. And soon as I hit the hall coming up to our door, I smell whatever it is she has cooking. She can make a whole meal on the hot plate, and we don't have but two pots. Still part of me feels like I've been robbed. I wanted to send for her. I wanted to have a house for her to come to. I wanted to have a business of my own . . .

I remember how I used to lean against that place in her, beyond her body, beyond touch, that was soft, like the spot at the top of a newborn's head, the place not completely formed. How it would take on my shape.

I crave a place like that, where nothing reaches, nothing calls my name; women I can satisfy. Women smelling of greens beneath a thin layer of cheap perfume, flesh sagging in rolls around their waists and behinds, supple, yielding.

But these images fall away like landscape, leaving behind that hollow-whistle yearning for fullness, the end of hunger.

*A reward with all reasonable expenses will be paid on delivering him to the Master of the Work-house . . .*

When will there ever be quiet, dreams that stop off somewhere?

No answer. Just the sweat and pant of my heart churning through darkness, steady as a wheel.

*My head will go willing,*
*but my heart will be obedient . . .*

# Iona 1945

i trace my life by the handprints i've collected    so many
    hands    i remember a dance    Elijah    fine pretty
    boy    chose me    i swam in color    in music
in the warmth of his mouth    yellow
    boy    prophet    mine    i waited for him by the
    window    waited to see him coming back to
    me    whispers in the sun tell me he gone    where you
    baby    miss
    you    waiting    waiting    baby    anything you got
i'll take    anything you want i got it    come on    home
baby    blkness eats a hole in me    losing water    losing
    blood    leaking    hope
a stranger's hands come to fix me    we met at church
    although we been knowing each other    for
    all my life    he smelled like bread    from the bakery
    he own
i let him take me    home
to his house    his wife dead    he had the same hole

inside    as me    that same    tunnel of need    i let him
pour me    scotch in a teacup    we sit up in his
parlor    on a stiff-backed
sofa covered in thick plastic    everything the way his wife
left it    i can't touch nothin in here    he pulls out a
dusty l.p.    my wife    never 'lowed    me to play my
records in here    but you iona
you look like a woman can handle the blues    sure i don't
mind 'em i say and reach
to pat my hair into place    the burn from the curling iron
swelling at the nape of my neck    my stockings
itch    he leans close    you smell so sweet baby
how 'bout some sugar for daddy    i give him my face
his kiss    all desperation and teeth
scotch burns the roof of my mouth    why don't we go
upstairs    he grins    i follow    flesh
like water beneath my girdle    he takes me    to the spare
room    not his wife's big bed
i undress    he undresses    lights on    we squeeze into the
twin bed    i have to turn
on my side to fit    he kneads me    soft dough    folding
beneath his fingers and i wonder which shape i would
take    hard roll    crescent-moon    his touch gentle
but unfamiliar
with the terrain of my body    unwilling to learn    but i am
thankful for kisses on my neck    the heart of his palm
circling my nipples    his other hand down there    i
wanna taste you    he bristles    between my thighs
my wife never let me see her    alternating thumb and
tongue    stiff hairs from his moustache prickling    he
enters me    and it is over before i can close my eyes
touch me baby    he whispers to the ceiling    i hold the soft
thing    you want me take you home now    yes thank

you    he turns his back to dress    doesn't offer
    the bathroom
we walk downstairs    blues still turning on the
    phonograph    the sound crunching beneath my
    feet    a road of glass    laid out for me to walk on
seem like    the length of    my life

his seed    was yeast in me    gave me my little girl    but he
    don't want neither of us
Anna say there's room in Chicago    so *I pack up my life and*
    *take it away.*

## Funeral Services Announced for Ms. Iona Jackson

Funeral Services for Ms. Iona Jackson, found murdered last week near Memphis, TN., will be held this Saturday morning at ten o'clock at Corpus Christi Church, 4920 South Parkway. Interment at Holy Sepulchre will follow.

A two-day wake, commencing this evening, will be observed in the home of Mrs. Agnes Lipsey, 2240 S. Calumet.

Ms. Jackson, entrepreneur and community activist, is survived by her daughter, Abella Jackson, 13; her aunt and uncle, Mr. and Mrs. Cedrick Wills, and a host of friends and associates. She will be dearly missed.

# Agnes 1958

Days after Iona's death, pondering the steps of my own journey, I begin to see the ways paths intersect and merge. The
letter from the City lies open on top of the bureau next to the
three jewelry boxes, overflowing with my rings, necklaces,
and bracelets. It covers the yellowing photographs stuck between the sheet of glass I had bought to protect the bureau's
top surface and the lace doilies underneath, which Mama
made for me when I first got the bedroom set, the first furniture that was mine, twenty years ago. Now the bureau is the
last thing anchoring me to this place.

They are taking my house to build another expressway. A
"fair settlement," their assessment of what the house is
worth, only a few hundred dollars more than I paid for it, is
waiting for me in a bank downtown. They had changed their
minds, again. Or maybe they always had this figured and I'm
just now being let in on the plan. The property they had used
up, deserted, and/or sold at inflated prices to the black folks
is now considered "prime," with its proximity to the lake and
downtown. They want it back.

But even two letters ago, it had been an idea, some distant maybe. Then my neighbors and I began to see white men poking around the neighborhood with tape measures and clipboards. And then nothing, a silence masquerading as relief. We had allowed ourselves to think that maybe they had decided that the highway they planned to build would be better situated somewhere else.

Looking back now, how could I have mistaken the quiet for calm? This is the second house they took from me. The first one and the businesses—my hotel, the poultry shop and chicken shack—were also lost to a highway. I suppose it's this basic faith, the belief in something unseen, unproven, that Negroes seemed to cultivate so well in their dealings with white people. It wasn't a faith in white folks per se, but rather a trust in the balance of the universe. *Why?* I recall the words of a young revolutionary whose voice shot through our radio and into the living room one evening, dividing everything in half. *Why should black people always be the ones to hold up the sky?*

Iona's face rushes through my memory, rattling my body like an empty house. We had both left the South wanting something. Iona called her something love, I called mine life. Even before I left Louisiana at sixteen, I could feel myself spiraling, drifting apart from the custom and routine in which my parents' lives were mired. I wanted my own life, something that I could shape as I saw fit. At first, when Iona passed, all I could see was the irony between us; how she was at rest while I was about to pick up and move again. But now I understand how movement and rest can sometimes be one and the same.

Each time I move, I manage to duplicate the arrangement of my things, like a garden that grows back each year stronger, so that every place feels like home. There is no way back, only forward motion, I console myself, leaving the room with only what my arms can carry.

# Anna 1958

We kept to the old ways: laying the body out in the house, the two-day wake. Although almost nobody held the wake at home anymore, everyone had gone along with it without question. It seemed right. No one could explain why at the time, for Iona had bent and shaped her life around the ways and demands of the city just like the rest of us. There was nothing to suggest that she would've preferred the old rite to the sleek, stylized services they had over at Leak's or one of the other popular funeral homes. But as I closed the door behind the last of the mourners draped in black, shades of white, gray, and blue, I began to understand.

Inside we had huddled together in Agnes's crowded parlor around the casket, or in the dining room around the table crowded with the dishes and parcels of food everyone had brought and deposited there even before removing their coats. The nostalgia, the remembering, had filled us up as much as the ham and chicken and sweet potato pie piled on our plates. In every corner there were tears and people talking shit, telling the kind of stories that gave our lives the height of the Loop's skyscrapers which could be seen from anywhere in Agnes's house. Stories some of us might have told when we went back home for the first time after moving to Chicago, except we were here. We were all here.

I listened as the talk turned to Iona, to the stories they told of her life and her death. Two boys had found her body, strangled and beaten, in a deserted house outside Memphis. She had just gotten engaged to Devil Franks, a local politician. He and Iona were traveling back to Waverly, Arkansas, Devil's hometown, to spend Thanksgiving with his family. Iona disappeared and was killed sometime during this trip. According to the one story they ran in the paper the murder was still unsolved.

"But you know Devil had to have a hand in it, if he didn't do it his self. He run with a rough crowd; know all them gangsters and policy kings. He coulda found somebody kill Iona for him. She had come up here and bought them rooming houses and those two laundries. Devil wanted to get him a piece a all that money." Iona's aunt, Viola Wills, stabbed the air with her index finger to punctuate her remarks, then crossed her arms over her chest and leaned back in her chair.

"But Viola, you know like I know, Iona don't have no sense when it comes to a man," a woman from the social club Iona had belonged to spoke up. "Iona would've given Devil everything she had."

"She must've have had some kind of sense, 'cause they still ain't found that money. Police say somebody went all through her houses looking for it. Tore up her stuff pretty bad," a cousin of Iona's added.

Viola leaned forward. "They ain't found it 'cause Iona put her money away a long time ago. Gave Abella everything, all the bank books and deeds to the property, to keep. Devil ain't getting a dime. And he know it. Why you think he didn't bother to show up to the wake today? That man is long gone." She leaned back in her seat again. A quiet fell over the room.

Cedrick Wills, Iona's uncle, ran his hand across the table, as if to wipe away all that had been said before. "Iona was just like everybody else up here," he broke the silence. "All she wanted was love she could call her own. She just wanted to belong to something, to be claimed by somebody."

We had stuck to the old ways, but we were no longer old-way people. Life had changed. People were moving away from the neighborhoods, out of the city. My youngest sister, Mabel, and her family had moved to California. Jack and I had moved to the house on Drexel and, although we kept in touch with the people we had known from church and the old neighborhood, there wasn't the same closeness. Agnes was about to lose her house to the City, for the second time, so that a new highway could be built. The kids, Marlene and Dennis, were in high school and didn't need me like they used to. We had changed.

I watched people leaving Agnes's that night, the way their bodies seemed lighter as they stepped into the cool afternoon, breathing out as though they had been holding their breath the whole time they were inside, gulping the dry air. They became like leaves catching wind. Today had been a last attempt at making sense of the nonsense of Iona's death, of our own lives, sometimes; a frenzied grasp at something more solid than brick, steel, mortar. Reaching back for the people we once were. I watched them gather their coats closer and cross their arms over their chests against the chill, then fold into long shiny cars.

There was no way back, I thought. We had lost our land in Louisiana. Mama and Daddy couldn't stand being so far away from their children after all of us moved North. They had moved to Chicago to be near us and just left the land behind. I heard that it was seized for taxes years ago. The roads were all highway now. You could drive and drive and speed right past the place where you were born. There was no place any-more: no house, no barn, no markers to tell you when it's time to slow down or stop.

I leaned against the warm side of the closed door. I could hear Agnes and Rowena in the kitchen and decided to go help them find a place for the mountains of leftovers that re-mained, despite our pushing heavy plates or bulky foil-wrapped packages into everybody's hands as they left. On my way back there, something drew me into the parlor, now empty except for the almost tangible stillness surrounding Iona's body. The silent rain of dust settling on the piano and coffee tables, the muted laughter spilling from the smiling lips of faces framed in photographs clustered on top the man-tel, the drone of a clock ticking, only approached and hov-ered at its fringes.

I dragged a chair through the thick air and sat down beside the coffin, at the end nearest Iona's head. This was the first time I had really seen her since they brought her body to the house this morning. I looked deep into my friend's face, at the lines around her eyes, snaking down her cheeks, barely visible beneath the layers of makeup caked on her skin. Which of these paths had led her here? How was it that just last weekend we would've been sitting up in this room, or back in the kitchen with Agnes and Rowena laughing before the three of them went out to Club DeLisa, their favorite night spot, and I went home to Jack and the kids? Now her eyes were sewn closed, her neck covered up in some old-maid high-collar dress to hide the bruises, her lips red and mo-tionless.

Iona had never been one of those red-lipped women hanging on the jukebox, sensuality emanating from them in invisible circular waves, commanding the space around them. But she wanted to be; to claim desire so openly, the maudlin promises of the love songs she collected made more tangible, more attainable, in the heat of a body pressed up against the machine. Iona was a lady, she followed the rules. She sat back and waited for the man who would love her to emerge out of the crowd with his hand and heart outstretched. She waited in the darkness of her empty houses, her heart flooded with a saltwater love that only increased her thirst. It was a dream she couldn't give up, the dream to which she had given everything.

I remembered those years of hunger, when Iona's need for love was so great it hurt me to look into her eyes, knowing that Iona, looking out into the world, at her own reflection, couldn't see anything that satisfied her. I couldn't help but wonder if this restlessness, her craving love so desperately, had been about Elijah all along; trying to fill that hole he left in her, needing somebody to say that she was good enough when Elijah and all the others had made her feel like shit. She wanted somebody to consume her; someone to live for when her own self, her accomplishments, even her daughter, were not enough.

She used to tell me how perfect she thought my life was, with Jack and the kids, the house. My life wasn't perfect. It was hard on Jack when I showed up in Chicago, announced only by the two-word postcard that I sent him a week before I left Warrior: "I'm coming." He had had this whole plan for how he thought things should go. He wanted to come here, start his business, get a house, and then send for me. Meanwhile, I was supposed to keep myself occupied and happy in Alabama waiting on him to be ready for me to be in his life again, full-time. This plan, selfish as it was, wasn't malicious on his part. It was about him trying to live up to his definition of a good man—providing for his family, being a husband and father who was there when we needed him—and at the same time achieve his own dream of having something of his own in this world. Jack expected perfection and grappled with the fact that, in his own judgment of himself, he always fell short.

I guess my coming here like I did was a reminder of all he hadn't done. It didn't help matters when, once I got to Chicago, I immediately went about constructing a life for myself. I went out with Agnes and Rowena, started taking a sewing class, got a little job at Agnes's hotel. I did everything at home that I had done before, as far as cooking and taking care of him and the house, but it wasn't the same. Jack wanted me the way I was when we first got married, when most of my energies were devoted to pleasing him, trying to keep him happy to insure that he would stay in love with me.

He wanted the woman who took whatever he had to give, who he could bend and shape according to his mood. He wasn't used to this new me who got cranky when it was hot and fussed at him for messing up the house, or let the rice burn if I was working on a new pattern, or asked him questions about where he was going and where he'd been.

There was a lot of tension between us during that first year or so, and I suspect there may have been other women, even after the baby was born. But, gradually, we began to settle into one another. Beyond all the troubles we were having, our love for one another kept us connected. It was no longer the urgent love we had when we first got married, or even the needful love, often unspoken, but which filled our letters to one another just the same. I missed the way we had been then, but the love we had once I moved to Chicago was probably the closest of all to freedom.

If you could draw a picture, this love would look like the letter V. We were joined at the root, each other's base, which gave us the strength to pursue our own lives. Jack eventually started his own business as a general contractor. He had a big account with a real estate mogul in the city and did all the painting and repairs in his buildings. This man helped us buy the house on Drexel. After that, Jack started a floral supply business and supplied most of the major flower shops in Chicago. He thought about buying the filling station where he worked for years, but never did.

I got a job at Mercy Hospital as a nurse's assistant in the maternity ward. And for the first time, I, too, felt like I had something that was all my own. I was proud of my work and I did it well. I was the only black woman down there that the white doctors and nurses would refer to by last name. Mrs. Dudley, they called me. The other black women couldn't stand it.

Occasionally that old tension between me and Jack would flare up. Sometimes he'd ask me for money to help cover the bills, and then resent the fact that he had to ask and that I had it to give. He didn't like that I kept my own money, and, more than this, that it had nothing to do with him. Sometimes he'd get back by not giving me a ride to work when he could have. But I took the bus most days anyway, leaving the house before it was light outside. I didn't like walking up to the stop in the dark, but slipping on my uniform in the morning, having some time to think on the bus, starting my day at the hospital, these were some of my greatest joys.

I wish you had found that joy in your life, Iona, God knows I do. My heart aches for you, girl. I already miss you. But, like we say, there is no going back. When I left Warrior and moved to Chicago, I left a lot of my life behind. I can't look back now. I suppose this is what happened to so many of us up here. We blended into the tall buildings and sidewalks, letting go of who we were back home in order to survive here, reinventing ourselves with each new day.

But sooner than I think, my children and my children's children will come knocking at my skin, their fingernails trying to make a mark, searching for a place that gives, opens like bread. And the hunger I see crusting at the corners of their mouths, hunger dry as cotton, will crystallize into questions about the past, about my life long ago. I will tell them that it was like a slow ship pulling away from the shore; how we learned to build our homes on water, and shed all heavy things in our wake.

# 2

# MARLENE

*Resurrection*

me being the oldest
i remember
the morning you woke up singing *I am I am*
the morning you held us to your chest
till all our cages opened and closed
rose and fell to the same rhythm
*we breathe one breath* you said *one breath*
me being the oldest
i remember
the day the sun never came
when you snatched us up and ran
to the night like an open flower folding
around us    a hand keeping secrets
hiding sweets asking *guess which? guess which?*
Breath then was a small sound    whispering
into your ever open ear *mama when?*
was scarce beneath the hay in the wagon
we figured had to be going somewhere
which only brought us back to nowhere
me being the oldest
i remember
it was a hard lash they brought down
on the smooth moon of your back

no woman's mercy     no hands
to cover the children's eyes     pull down the skirt
snatched over your head     dab a little at the blood
and the dying came quick     i could tell
but i reached up and caught you     right before
you had the chance
to close us out of your eyes and float away
we are a strange season     colored folks
dying     and returning to die some more
but i caught you     still in bloom
and my arms will be the place
where breathing comes easy     my chest
the rise and fall of a familiar morning song
the rhythm that waits for you to find it
to take back what you've given
the small voice whispering
*life life life*

Dr. W. B. Martin
Warrior, Ala.
December 30, 1944

Dear Jack,

The greeting was received with joy. Sure
is a fine looking Baby. She look very much
like Herbert little girl Carrie Louann. We
all are very glad to have her picture in our
home on the Piano looking out at every one.
I am coming to Chicago this spring or summer
to bring Carrie to see all. We would not
take a million for her and I am sure we will
Be the same about your Marlene. Had a letter
from Al he is fine. Says write him he has a
new address

Cpl. Albert Dudley
36171823
Co. B. 383 Engr Bn
A.P.O. 507
N.Y., N.Y.

So Write him Please.
Robert has his honorable discharge so he
is home. We had a very nice Xmas hope you
had the same. Hope Annie Mae and baby are
fine. Tell her to write some time.

Love to all from your Mother,

Mrs. A. Dudley

# Marlene 1995

*This road has our name on it . . .*

Daddy's voice reaches for me, like a hand shooting through darkness to graze the skin of my bare arms, numb from the cold pouring out of vents lining the walls of Logan airport. His voice, clear, as though he were here speaking to me, was the first thing, besides the cold, that I could feel.

God, I'm ready for the seasons to change, the teasing heat of May not enough to melt away layers of winter imbedded in my skin. Sick of things in transition and beginnings, I hunger for summer, that moment when everything finishes growing, blossoming, changing, and stands still. The memory of Daddy's voice felt like that; like somebody breathing warm on me, the hot circle of air that would rise from my children's mouths, branding my neck, arms, nipples as they nursed or slept.

How long has it been since I held them close like that? Since they were tiny squirming things wrapped secure in my arms? I couldn't keep them there, no matter how I tried, still try. They had grown legs which, these days, seem to send them bounding further and further away from me, and hands which reach for something other than what I can offer, even though I've offered everything. I have risked my life and given it to become a mother. No. Can't go back there. Thinking about my children, the four of them scattered in three different states, reminds me too much of what I have been trying all morning to forget: motion, leavings, loss.

I close my eyes against these thoughts, against the cold, and the glaring white light from fluorescent lamps like illuminated tunnels overhead.

*A flush of dark crimson behind my eyes becomes the night. An indigo sky as deep as water fills our car as Mama, Daddy, my brother, Dennis, and I skim the endless road, wide and flat as an open palm, on our way to Alabama.*

*This road has our name on it . . .*

. . . was what he said every time, as we turned away from the city onto the narrow two-lane highway that would take us all the way to Warrior—the small town where Daddy was born, and where his parents and most of his sisters and brothers still lived and worked on the family farm. Behind us, Chicago's bright lights and noise blurred into a ball the size of my thumbnail, shimmering in the distance like a tiny solitary star.

*There I am . . . curled up beside Dennis in the back seat of the Buick, with its two fingers of pale yellow-white light poking into the darkness. My feet don't reach the floor. Up front, where Mama and Daddy sit, is another country.*

*"How's my navigator?" Daddy turns to ask me over his*

*shoulder. He has given me the maps to hold, like always. "You
not sleeping on the job back there, are you?"*

*"No, Daddy, I'm awake. See. I'm up." I stretch my lids wide
so that he can see the whites of my eyes in the rear-view mirror.
"Good. Can't have my navigator sleeping on me. You s'posed
to be charting the course." I smile, knowing that the maps in my
hand now would probably end up stuffed into the glove compart-
ment or the trunk on the way back, unused. Daddy didn't need
me to tell him how to get there. He could make this trip in his
sleep, he's done it so many times. We make the day-and-a-half-
long drive every July or August. For us, Alabama is the roundness of summer, our visit like a mountain peak and all the other
days a slow climb to the top and then a fast slide down.*

There was a science to those rides, a ritual, a magic, all
their own. Just as Muslims wash before prayer, and Chris-
tians are baptized in holy water before being allowed into the
kingdom of Heaven, we made our own preparations to go
"home." A week before we left, Mama would start us cleaning the house. "Nothing worse than coming home to a nasty
house," was the phrase we heard so often during that week, it
could've been enshrined on one of those wooden plaques and
hung above our front door, the Dudley Family Motto. Dennis and I could barely sit down or touch anything before
Mama would come wiping up behind us. And we didn't have
Daddy to appeal to, for most days during that week he would
leave the house early in the morning, before we were awake,
to open his little store—really more like a stand—where he
sold fresh vegetables and live chickens. He wouldn't get home
until late, sometimes after we had gone to bed.

But the night before we were to leave, we all came together
again. All of us in the kitchen, jazz or country and western
belting out of the radio. Me, Dennis, and Daddy sitting at the

table, Mama standing up by the stove. Daddy's foot tapping in his big black shoes. The smell of the chicken Mama always fried for our trip mingling with the scent of new ink rising up from Daddy's maps.

Every summer was the same. Daddy would buy the maps and study them for hours. "Let's say we try a different route this time," he'd turn to me, running his fingers along the tangle of red, blue, black, and yellow lines. But despite the hours he spent plotting alternative routes, the Buick, as though driving itself, would end up at the road where, for us, the trip to Alabama always began, just as the last bit of sun faded behind clouds thickening into night.

*As we drive, our city skins fall away with the miles, like shedding so many layers of winter clothing, until, finally, we feel as light as the breeze coming through our open windows. Mama hands Daddy a cigarette, its lighted tip the sun of our faraway tomorrow rising at the other end of the highway, over the narrow, dirt lane—almost a road itself—leading to Nanny and Dad's big brick farmhouse, and, beyond that, the land that goes on so long it turns to sky. We will drive all the way to the part where gravel ends and grass begins, alongside the house right by the kitchen. All of our relatives—my grandparents, Nanny and Dad, Uncle Herbert, Shorty, Cousin Carrie, Uncle Buddy— will be there to meet us, streaming out of the kitchen door to engulf us in a wave of hugs and kisses before Daddy can turn off the engine.*

*Ahead of us are mornings of waking to rooster crows, the smell of bacon and Nanny's biscuits, the heavy drum of men's footsteps—Daddy's among them—as they go to meet the field and their day's work, the laughter of women falling like rain. I will ride with Nanny on her milk wagon as she makes her deliveries in town, pleased as the sun turns my pale skin brown as bread. In* the evenings, Carrie and I will comb Dad's soft, white, shoulder-length hair and think of snow, but warm.

The long stretch in between Chicago and Alabama, though, is ours alone. We belong only to each other. No more work, no more school, nothing keeps us apart. Out here, in the dark, my leg blends into my brother's hand, the front seat, Daddy's shoulders seeming to span the width of the car, Mama's hair lifting in the wind. The hum of tires skimming warm concrete becomes a second heartbeat.

Night is a keeper of secrets. The air then is thick with words people have sealed away from sound and those that have belted out, escaped. Somewhere in between there are prayers. I am thinking this as Daddy pulls over onto the road's gravel shoulder so that we can go to the bathroom and eat. In the 1940s and '50s, the roads are still a dangerous place for people like us, but we don't know it. Dennis and I explode from the car, rushing into the dark of an endless field.

"Marlene! Dennis! Don't go too far! You all wait for me!" Mama's voice trails behind us, struggling to keep up. But we're too fast, too far. We run until our legs burn, until we feel completely on our own. Night is a keeper of secrets; I have the feeling we are one of them.

Back at the car, Mama has unpacked the food and has a plate waiting for each of us. Dennis and I perch on top of the warm hood. Daddy stretches the full length of the front seat and Mama sits in the back, sideways, with her legs hanging out.

When we start driving again, Mama and Daddy's hushed voices form a circle around the two of them. They become Anna and Jack, the couple in the pictures taken before I was born. I fall asleep listening to the soft rustle of their whispers and private laughter, seeing a reflection of myself on the window in the light of an oncoming car, thinking how, against this night, my own eyes could be stars.

Once, as an adult, I referred to our Alabama trips as a vacation. Daddy immediately corrected me. "Home is not a vacation," he said. "Home is a whole other life." I have come to know this well. Everyone has their own Alabama. We live in the long stretch in between; the space, the balance, you're constantly negotiating between where you come from and where you think you're going. And one is always tugging at the other. Except, for me, there are no more roads, no well-worn routes.

All the roads have turned to sky.

Sky is tenuous. Nothing to hold. No signs to count down the miles, to tell you how far you've come and how much is left to go. You can lose your way up there, in the flat endlessness of sky. Its enormity both engulfs and negates your presence at the same time.

The airport was deserted when I first arrived; just me and the morning cleaning crew to share the cavernous room. I remember thinking that the emptiness felt like sky.

*Mama's taken a turn. They're telling everybody to come . . .*

I had noticed the heaviness in my chest as soon as I opened my eyes yesterday morning and then felt a slow panic begin to crawl up my back, as though something was unraveling from the base of my spine. I lay still, staring blankly at the ceiling, traveling my body inwardly searching for pain. There wasn't any that I could recognize, no throbbing, cramping, or strain; no constellation of symptoms to be noted or accounted for in the haphazard attempt to give whatever this was a name. There was nothing. Nothingness spreading over every inch of my body.

I kept waiting for the panic to blossom, expecting it any second to wrap around me and stop my breath. I even balled my hands into fists, preparing for the moment when my heart would explode. Still nothing. It was as though part of me had separated from the rest. The frame of my body remained intact, but inside the detached part just hung suspended.

*Call Mama,* something urged. *Marlene, call Mama.* It wasn't the words that I heard, but a rush of sound welling up and swirling around my eardrums, like waves echoing in the hollow of a seashell. Instinctively, I heaved over onto my side, reaching for the phone. But as soon as I moved, I fell back, all of my strength drained that quick. I couldn't bring myself to do it, to dial the number to Mama's hospital room, which, in the three months she had been there, had become as familiar as Mama's home phone. The tightness in my chest felt like all of the bones of my rib cage had been braided together into a knot. I recognize it now for what it was: a message, warning, omen.

There have always been people in my family who could sense the future through their bodies—an itching hand, a sore knee, a heavy heart—although, they couldn't necessarily name it. My grandfather, Papa, Mama's daddy, had been known for his visions and dreams. Mama told me that when she was a little girl in Louisiana the nuns in their parish would call Papa down to the church, sit him in a little room, and have him tell them his dreams. The only one of Papa's dreams that Mama remembered was the one about the cypress branch, a mourning symbol. After Papa had that dream, Mama's baby sister died, "before she was even walking good." The few times I can remember Mama or one of my aunts telling this story it always ended like this:

"The child left this world before she even had a name," they'd lament. "Or maybe she did have a name and just nobody thought to use it. Maybe we knew what would happen to her somehow. We all just called her Baby." Then there was Mama's power to see right through me. The day before my thirteenth birthday, Mama and I were in the kitchen finishing up the preparations for my party. Suddenly, Mama looked up and told me that she would know if I had sex, if I even thought about it. This alone had frightened me enough to keep me from even imagining too hard the strange words and sounds and movements I believed the deceptively small package of that three-letter word must contain.

Mama's power was proven again and again. She had known it the time in my junior year of high school I let my boyfriend, Ben, hold me so close I lost my heartbeat. A year later, Mama had known it the Sunday I almost died. She sensed the exact moment the city bus had come careening into the side of the car, stealing the life of one of my best friends and fracturing my body like one of Dennis's puzzles spread out on the dining room table. One minute we were making plans to go to the Regal Theater, and the next, it was night inside my head and quiet, too quiet. Mama said she had felt a shock run through her legs, that's how she had known. She felt this pain in her legs for three months, the time it took me to learn to walk again.

When I had my own kids, I was amazed that I, too, had the power to read them, especially my daughters. Their skin, whenever they were trying to hide something, turned translucent as rice paper and I could peel thin layer by thin layer, all the way to the glowing light of their hearts . . .

Yesterday morning when I finally got out of bed and opened the blinds to let the sun in, I pressed my hands against the glass, wanting to feel the warmth I found there all over. I called Mama when I got to work.

"They brought me back over here," Mama whispered, defeated. Mama had recently decided to have an operation to unclog the arteries in her legs—the result of previous bypass surgery. The doctors told us that her chances of surviving this latest operation were extremely low, but Mama had pulled through it. A few weeks later, they took her out of the Intensive Care Unit and put her into the hospital's rehabilitation center. My aunt Agnes and I had been there, just a few weeks ago, helping her with her physical therapy. Mama looked good, stronger than she had looked in years. Her spirits were up. The doctors had even given us a date when she could go home. This morning, right before my call, they had transferred Mama back to Intensive Care.

"You're going to be fine, Mama," I tried to reassure her. "They just want to check your breathing to make sure everything's okay." I hadn't spoken with the doctors yet, but even I didn't believe what I was saying, although I prayed for it to be true. "I'm going to call the doctors . . ."

Mama sighed. "I can't talk right now." I could barely hear her.

"I love you, Mama. I'll call you back . . ." Someone hung up the phone before I could finish. The knot in my chest got tighter. I left work soon after I talked to Mama and the doctors, then walked the long way to the subway station, the sun hugging my body.

I wasn't surprised when the phone rang around two this morning, waking me out of the deep sleep I had fallen into as soon as I got home from work. Dennis's voice was on the other end, *Mama's taken a turn . . . They're telling everybody to come.* I don't remember making my airline reservations, but I remember getting here three hours early for my flight; the steady way my daughter, Nicole, my second child, held the wheel on the drive to the airport, like an adult. My daughter was grown, I thought, as though seeing this for the first

time. I made her promise not to have me paged at the airport
if there was any news from the hospital.

"I don't want to know anything," I had said, getting out of
the car. I remember talking briefly with Mama's doctor before we left the house. *Tell Mama I'm coming*, I'd instructed,
sensing that, somehow, Mama already knew.

*Once I knew the secret of spiraling inward, finding a place
within myself where nothing could reach.* I was eight or nine
when I discovered it. We were living in the building on 49th
and Vincennes, a tenement, although, as far as I knew, nobody who lived there ever thought of it that way.

We had loved each other then. Black folks. Maybe because
we had to in those close quarters. All of us packed together on
the South Side and more coming from down South. Most of
the buildings, like ours, had been chopped up into small
apartments. There were entire families squeezed into apartments which, in whiter and more prosperous times, had been
single rooms. But even in those cramped black neighborhoods of the forties and fifties, thrown together as we were,
there was also that part of us —there must have been—that
loved one another because we wanted to. Freely, recklessly.
You could feel it in the energy of crowded streets, wide with
possibility, bodies still so close; in the way people spoke the
names of stores and hangouts as intimately as those of children and lovers.

A love undergirded by rest, guarded by women like weep-
ing willows, all arms, hanging from windows and porches,
reaching out to encircle this world in their embrace; men like
scarecrows perched on small squares of grass in front of the
great stone buildings they didn't own, but claimed as their
own nonetheless.

Our apartment had three rooms, one of the largest units in

the building. But to me and Dennis, those three rooms could have been twenty. My favorite place in the house was our bathroom. From wherever I was, I would go there, slipping into the shade of the empty room like a whisper to join its stillness. Behind me the door would close with a soft click, shutting out the world. I poured myself into the narrow space between the bathtub and the sink. This is where I came to read, to dream, to be alone with my thoughts; where I brought the pieces of myself for which there was no place in my life on the other side of that door.

*As the coolness of black and white tiles seeped into the back of my thighs, making them stick to the floor, I would watch the last of the afternoon, a pie-slice of sun, slide across the tile and up the side of the tub, then disappear into its deep valley. Soon the wedge of light emerged on the other side, crept up the wall and finally vanished out of a small square window with its shade half-drawn. Then, I closed my eyes.*

*That day, as I sank into the quiet, waiting for Mama to come home, I was thinking only of the crisp white booklets tucked deep in the outside pocket of my school bag. Raffle tickets for this year's Pastors' Tea. Earlier that afternoon, Father Joseph had visited my seventh grade class to announce the event, which Corpus Christi, our church, hosted every fall.*

*"Each Corpus Christi family is expected to sell at least five books of chances," Father instructed. "The young man and the young woman who sell the most raffle tickets will be crowned King and Queen of the Pastors' Tea, and . . ." Father paused, holding up two books of tickets, "will each win a new Schwinn bicycle!" Father beamed around the room, his pale blue eyes skimming the small brown faces raised expectantly as the words sank in, his own white skin flushed red at the cheeks.*

*"Who wants to win?" he bellowed, picking up the small*

*brown box which contained the raffle tickets. Every hand in the
room shot up, except mine. But I was probably the one who
wanted most to win, so badly I could feel the ache in my teeth
from my heart punching against my rib cage, a bird trying to
break through bone.*

I know what it's like to feel yourself split into two, to live
in between. I was always aware of these two sides of myself:
The one girl who believed what her mother told her, that she
was beautiful and smart and special, who lived firmly
grounded in the knowledge Mama planted in the valley beneath her tongue, the depth of her own worth. And then
there was the girl in me who turned from this place and, instead, pressed her face against the window-eyes of strangers,
hoping to catch a glimpse of her reflection.

It was this girl's tears that fell on the days I came home
from school crying when the kids teased me. This girl saw
only the faults other people were quick to show her and hungered for something she could not name. This girl Mama
scolded: "You are too sensitive. Why give people so much
power? If they find out they can hurt you, they'll just keep
clawing away at your weakness until they tear you apart.
People feed off of pain and misery. How many times do I have
to tell you? You don't ever let anybody get inside of you like
that."

It was this girl's heart racing toward the crown when Father Joseph announced the Pastor's Tea; who sat dreaming of
the girl she would become if she were queen. All those eyes
on her, all those arms reaching out to pull her closer . . .

*"Dear God, please let me be queen." Uttering this quick
prayer, I left the bathroom and hurried to the small alcove off of
our kitchen, to the window where I could look out and see Mama*

*coming home. I knelt on the wooden bench next to the phone, arms folded on the windowsill. Outside, a steady stream of folks just getting off from work emerged out of a blaze of orange sky. The smell of other people's food and fuel lingering on skin and hair, the specks of blood from the slaughterhouses and grime missed cleaning up after the whistle, the stale scent of exhaustion, merged here with the smell of their own dinner cooking, children's cries, the perfumed anticipation of love later on.*

*Uniforms, belonging to maids, doctors, gas station attendants, funeral home owners, secretaries, doormen, cooks, chauffeurs, dentists, nurses, shoe shine boys, writers, carpenters, lawyers, were a season unto themselves. Winking gold-plated buttons were slowly undone. Arms and hands rose in arcs to slide off caps and aprons. Lunch pails rattled empty against knees and thighs. Entering the street, the walkers gained momentum, having spilled from buses on South Parkway (now King Drive), two blocks away. The swish of doors closing behind them cut them loose for these few brief hours. Cars turning onto the block this time of evening parked, motors slept until morning.*

*Every now and then, a familiar face would look up and see me in the window, mostly people from our building. Rosemary, from down the hall, passed by dressed in her zebra print miniskirt and matching top, which highlighted every curve of her body, a huge white cowboy hat perched on her head, and knee-high cowboy boots with tall, spikey heels. All eyes were on her as the men on the block followed her slow swaying hips and the women turned away in envy masked as disgust. Although I had heard people speak of her as one, Rosemary was "not a prostitute." She was "a shake dancer" who entertained at local clubs. She was also, she would proudly tell you, the "first black woman dancer down at the race track." She lived in a one-room apartment with her daughter, where everything was painted a shade of pink.*

*There was Ms. Bryant, who lived by herself next door to us, although she always had her men-friends coming over to see her.*

She kept her radio playing. Music seeped through the walls and beneath her door. But on the days her company came, another kind of music filled her room and spilled out into the hallway: the scent of his cologne, the deep rumble of his voice, the high-pitched trill of her laugh . . .

Mama didn't allow us to visit either of these women, not even Ms. Bryant, and she was friends with her, although Mama never went inside her apartment either.

There was Smitty, who sold peanuts and snow cones on the corner, packing up his cart for the day. Mr. Gail, the super, sweeping around the building. And finally, there was Mama, plump in her white nurse's aide uniform, among the last walking from the bus. I saw her stop to talk with a woman from across the street. Come on, Mama, hurry up, I urged through the window, tempted to tap on the glass. When I saw her turn away and wave goodbye to her friend, I rushed to the front door and flung it open, sticking my head out to watch her walking down the hall.

"Mama, I need to talk to you," I called before she reached our apartment.

"Can I please get in the house first?" Mama sighed with mock exasperation. I stepped aside to let her through the door.

"Now can we talk, Mama?"

"What's your rush, girl!? At least let me pull off my clothes and get comfortable." I followed her through the living room, which doubled as her and Daddy's bedroom, and watched as she peeled off the white low-heeled nurse's shoes, the white stockings, the knee-length white dress which buttoned down the front. She hung up and put away each piece of clothing in turn, then slipped on the loose flower-print dress she wore around the house.

"Your Daddy bring a chicken up from the stand?" she asked on her way to the kitchen. I shrugged. "What about the beans? Did you remember to turn them on when you got home?" I nodded, yes.

"Good," Mama said both to me and to the raw chicken,

*wrapped in brown paper, that Daddy had left on the countertop. Mama transferred the bundle to the sink and began cutting the chicken into parts.*

*"What was it you needed to talk about so badly?" Mama glanced over her shoulder at me. The words tumbled out of my mouth.*

*"Father Joseph handed out raffle tickets today, the ones we have to sell for the Pastor's Tea. Whoever sells the most gets to be king or queen and wins a bicycle. I want to be queen, Mama. I want to be the one up there in front of everybody. Show those stupid girls at school always bothering me . . ."*

*Mama opened her mouth about to speak, then changed her mind and closed it. But the way she looked at me, it was like she was staring inside, through my skin, at my two trembling selves.*

*"I really, really want to win, Mama. I have to . . . but I know I can't sell all those tickets. I'm not good at stuff like that."*

*"Maybe there's some other way we can do it." Mama turned back to her chicken.*

*"Yeah, but how?" I pressed. Mama was quiet for a moment, then she whirled around to face me, knife suspended.*

*"Maybe we could sell dinners. Chitlins or fried chicken with spaghetti and slaw, something like that. We could make it so that the price of the raffle ticket is included in the meal, so each dinner we sell, we also sell a ticket."*

*"Ooh Mama! You think we can do it?" I squealed, dancing around the kitchen, the way to the crown opening before me.*

*The rest of the week and part of the next was spent collecting orders. Mama tacked up signs at Daddy's stand and at church. Dennis and I enlisted our friends and went door to door in our building and around the neighborhood.*

*The day the dinners were to be prepared and delivered, Daddy left the house before sunrise and drove his truck to Indiana to pick up a fresh load of chickens. Mama took the day off from work and got up with Daddy to start cooking. By the time I got home from school, the house was filled with the smell of fried chicken and chitlins; with laughter competing with bodies for space in our kitchen. I hung back in the doorway, just watching the scene. Everyone I knew was there. My aunt Agnes was turning the chicken and stirring the huge boiling pots of chitlins and spaghetti. Aunt Rowena was cutting vegetables and opening cans of tomatoes for the spaghetti sauce. Ms. Bryant was sitting at the kitchen table, doing more talking than work. Mama was everywhere at once, wrapping dinners for those who had dropped by to pick them up, getting salt and pepper and drinks for the few who were eating already, paper plates balanced on their palms and knees.*

*But in the midst of all this, the chaotic laughter, the chatter rising and falling in unpredictable waves, there was order. Somewhere beneath it all, everyone's voice, the cooking smells and sounds, joined in a single purpose. It was all for me.*

*The day I was crowned Queen of the Pastor's Tea, the following Sunday, we arrived at church early to help set up the seventh-grade table. People kept stopping by to tell Mama how much they had enjoyed her dinners and what a good daughter I was, how smart we were to come up with the idea. I was so proud and pleased with the attention that I wasn't even thinking about the moment the winners would be announced. When my name was called, I looked at Mama and started to hug her, but she pushed me toward the stage at the front of the auditorium. I remember when the pastor draped the robe over my shoulders, the heaviness of the red crushed velvet. The crown, though, was lighter than I expected.*

*That night, Mama came into the room Dennis and I shared and sat on my bed. She asked me if I was happy, and I said, yes. Then Mama told me that she had known it all along.*

*"What?" I asked.*

*"You being queen," she answered.*

*"How did you know we would sell all those dinners?" I asked.*
*"I'm not talking about the dinners. I'm talking about you be-*
*ing queen. I knew it all along, but I wanted you to see for*
*yourself."*

This is how I came to be queen, possessor of the key to my
own kingdom. A gift from Mama, one it took me many years
to open, and even longer to know how to use.

"Good morning, ladies and gentleman. We are now ready
to begin boarding our nonstop flight to Chicago O'Hare . . ."
The static from the PA system jolts me from memory. My
heart starts its frantic pounding and I hold my breath, half-
expecting my name to be called, or the ticket agent to approach me and lead me away to deliver the awful news. *It's*
*about your mother,* she would say. I close my eyes and wait for
the next sharp crackle of static that would bear my name, the
gentle tapping fingers. When there is only the hurried rustle
of the other passengers collecting themselves and their belongings, I stand up to join the line to board the plane. And,
for a moment, I don't know where I am. Chicago. Boston. *So*
*many leavings and comings, all the places blend into one.* Without realizing it, I have raised my arms slightly, reaching out
to gather my kids around me. Just like the days when we traveled as a unit, the five of us huddled together, moving in a
cluster up to the ticket podium, where I would hand the agent
our tickets and wait for him to count them and confirm that
we were all there. *So many leavings . . .*

As I walk through the door and into the tunnel leading to
the plane, I remember how one of the kids, joking around—
Omar I think it was—once called this the point of no return.

When we are airborne, I lift the plastic shade covering the
narrow dome-shaped window and stare into a seamless blue

sky. *I always thought I would be the one who stayed. Forgive me, Mama. Forgive me.* The words come back, the same tireless refrain I've hummed every day of the ten years I've been gone. The moment of my leaving, clear in my memory, replays itself each time I get on a plane.

I never wanted to leave home. I couldn't even envision myself anywhere else. Dennis was the one who seemed to need to carve out his own space away from home, not me. I couldn't imagine leaving Mama and Daddy, the comfort of my family. That's just how I thought of myself, defined myself, even after I was gone.

When my husband, Herman, died, I just wanted to pick up and move, fly away somewhere. I took the kids to Europe that first summer without him. Me alone with four young children traipsing around the world, what was I thinking? But even Europe didn't feel far away enough, because, eventually, I had to come back home, and no matter where I went the dreams would find me. Nightmares in which I could feel him tugging at me, his hands decayed down to the bone, trying to pull me into a dark place. In the beginning, the touch was hungry, desirous, reminding me of those nights we wanted each other so badly, we could only speak with our hands, clutching and tearing away at one another's clothing, the sweet tangle of limbs.

But as the dream progressed, his touch would grow more insistent.

"Our kids are still here, Herman," I would plead with him in my sleep. "They have to live. They need me, honey." The hands would keep tugging, grabbing hold of anything they could—my nightgown, breasts, ankles. I would lose my voice. After what felt like hours of struggling, I'd be able to utter, in a raspy, barely audible whisper, "Leave me alone," and the dream ended as suddenly as it began. I would force myself awake, feeling winded and sore, unbalanced, but thoroughly convinced that I had just saved my life.

> after he died
> what really happened is
> she watched the days
> bundle into thousands,
> watched every act become
> the history of others,
> every bed more
> narrow . . .
> she walked away
> from the hole in the ground
> deciding to live. and she lived.

. . . away from the days, the long waking hours, that felt more like dreaming. My life didn't seem real anymore, didn't feel like mine. My family, my friends, everybody, started to treat me as though I had died with Herman. I was supposed to be the widow, stay at home with the kids, grieve for Herman *and* depend on them for everything. This meant that I was also subject to their judgment and criticism on anything from how I dressed to how I raised my kids. I was supposed to give up my existence, become who they thought I should be, but no one was really offering anything in return. They wanted their say in how I lived my life, but, when I needed something, they were only available when they wanted to be.

Worst of all, no one seemed to fully appreciate the significance of the loss we had sustained. After the initial shock of Herman's death wore off, things quickly returned to normal, as though nothing had happened.

"But my kids no longer have a father in their lives! I am without the man I love!" I always seemed to be on the brink of screaming. There was nobody to fill that void for my kids. By the time Sonny died—that's what they called Herman, always the center, the life of any party or conversation—the number of men in our family had dwindled to a handful. My daddy had passed shortly after Tasha, my first child, was born. Gone too, were the uncles and cousins and men from the neighborhood I had grown up around. They had died or scattered like birds frightened from their perch . . .

Still, it wasn't just what was happening with the family. It was me, too. Me trying to explain this inexplicable thing that had happened. Me trying to figure out who I was if not wife any longer; how I was going to maintain the same lifestyle for the kids that Herman had provided for us as a family. Me, the one who was supposed to stay, rationalizing these wings suddenly beginning to sprout, this overwhelming urge to leap.

*"Boston?" Mama winced as though she had just been slapped.*

*"Well, that's where the school is, Mama." It was June, 1985. My husband had been dead almost two years. Mama and I were sitting at the kitchen table talking. I had just told her of my plans to move to Boston at the end of the summer. I was going back to school, to Harvard, for my masters.*

*"And the kids? After what they've been through, you're just going to take them away from their friends and school? From everything they know?"*

*"The kids'll be fine. The schools are good in Cambridge, probably better than here. They'll adjust, make new friends. I'm a little worried about Tasha, though. She doesn't want to leave her friends, and I don't blame her. She's been with that same group of kids since nursery school, and now they're starting high school. . . . But I know she'll be okay, too. The change might do us all some good."*

*"What about all these universities in Chicago? I thought you*

were going to look into some of them. None of them are good enough?" Mama, her face creased in the same pained expression.

"Mama, I looked into the schools here. You know I did," I said, gently, pleading with her to understand. "It's just that Harvard has the best program for what I want to do." The truth was, I had visited Cambridge and fallen in love with the place. Even though the thought of leaving home pained me, it had always been a dream of mine to go away to school. Cambridge, Harvard Square in particular, was everything like my fantasy. It was quaint cobblestone sidewalks and street musicians, exotic restaurants and artsy boutiques, students with backpacks on their shoulders, intellectuals reading or talking over coffee at outdoor cafés, at least five bookstores within a couple of blocks of one another. And Harvard itself, here was a place I could use my mind, engage in heavy conversations and debate, share ideas.

However, soon after our arrival, I discovered that my idealized vision of Cambridge was a reality only for white folks. We had to put up with the same racist bullshit as anywhere else—people bumping into you in the stores like you weren't there, professors dismissing your ideas and/or stealing them. There was even a beggar, a fixture in "the Square," who would call every black person 'nigger' as they passed. But that night, as Mama and I talked, Cambridge was the only place I thought I could become this new self I felt announcing herself.

The day we left was storming. Mama had arranged for her brother, my uncle J.B., who owned a limousine service, to take me and the kids to the airport in one of his cars. All that morning, Mama and I avoided one another's eyes, doing last-minute packing and cleaning while the kids sulked around the house. What did we say to each other those last few hours? It couldn't have been anything much, nothing about my leaving. It would be years before we could talk about that.

*Mama stood at the top of the stairs on the front porch, watching as we loaded all of our luggage into the back seat and trunk of the limousine. She had decided not to ride with us to the airport. When it was time to go, the kids ran up to give her last-minute hugs and kisses. I hung back, waiting for a moment alone with her. I had decided that I would say something; tell her I didn't mean to hurt her, that leaving was the only way I felt I could live my life. But when that moment came, the arguments which had seemed so compelling, so solid in my mind, fell apart as I looked into her face, contorted the way it had been that night in the kitchen: the disbelieving mouth, eyes red with surrender, grief settling deep into the folds of her cheeks, and anger.*

*Yes, there was anger, but I would only discover this when my own face began to take on a similar countenance, as, one by one, my kids left home. You feel robbed somehow; as if somebody had rummaged through your house, fingered all of your belongings and taken everything of value, leaving behind the distinct impression—in the careless way things are flung about—that even your best wasn't good enough.*

*What I remember most about that day is the funereal crawl of the limousine pulling away from the house; Mama, still on the porch, waving occasionally after the car. I would relive this scene again and again in my memory, and at the end of every visit home . . .*

I always thought I would be the one who stayed. *Forgive me, Mama.* Could there have been another way? The question emerges suddenly. Could I have made another life in Chicago? Could I have stayed? *Mama, I'm sorry.* I could've stayed. What would it have taken? I could've stayed. All the so-called freedom and independence wasn't worth the pain of leaving. *I never forgave myself, Mama, even after you did.* I left when Mama's health was beginning to deteriorate. I pulled my kids out of school, and we became nomads, all of us. How unthinkable it must have been, my leaving, when Mama and Daddy had moved their entire lives so that we could rest.

As the plane nears the ground, the city where I was born opens up to welcome me into its embrace once again. After all this time, I still don't think of Boston as home. It's like home, familiar, comfortable, but whenever I talk about the place I feel the need to qualify, to explain. "I *live* in Cambridge, but I'm *from* Chicago." As though just these words, the adamant pledge of allegiance, make the years I've been away seem shorter, my leaving less like a betrayal.

Landing always feels the same: the flush of excitement and relief at my first glimpse of the flat, gray landscape with its box-shaped bungalows and small patches of green; the grid-work of city streets, neighborhoods, which, true to Chicago's reputation as one of the most segregated cities in the country, seem sharply delineated and divided even from the air. It is not a ceremonious arrival. I find this to be reassuring in ways, almost as if I had never left. But each time I return, I see that the city has grown and expanded without me. Buildings and houses have been torn down, stores closed, new structures added in their place, or, quite often, just the vacant lot is left to testify, to witness the stories and memories of everyone who was once connected to that place.

*Forgive me, Mama. Forgive me.*

Outside the airport, my sister-in-law is waiting for me in her car. It could've been Herman sitting beside me. We could've been on our way to the hospital for one of the babies to be born. Or maybe at the beginning of one of our family excursions: a nighttime drive to Memphis to visit the relatives on his side; or to Wisconsin for a weekend at the Abbey, the resort we both loved in Lake Geneva, and then the elaborate brunch we treated ourselves to Sunday morning at the Play- boy Club before heading home.

Yes, those were his gangly legs folded beneath the wheel. And the hands . . . You could see the strength rippling be- neath his taut mahogany skin, the surprising delicacy of the lithe, curving fingers. Hands, which, every time he touched me, especially in the beginning, seemed capable of holding my entire body, as though all of me could fit in the shallow bowl of his palms and it would be no weight at all.

The old songs, the jazz standards we loved, the velvet night outside, would fill the car with a sweetness that was al- most tangible; something I could taste, or wrap around my shoulders against the nighttime chill. By now the kids would be asleep in the back seat, and we would ease into that sacred space beneath the music, the doorway to our other selves. We metamorphosed, the way Mama and Daddy had in the dark- ness during those Alabama rides, becoming again the wide- eyed lovers staring out at the future like an empty stretch of road, every sidelong glance a seduction, each kiss a prayer for forever, each caress an awesome discovery, everything possi- ble, everything ours and impossible to lose.

Herman and I met in the living room of my parents' house. He and Dennis both belonged to the same social club, and, on this particular afternoon, Dennis had invited Herman and the rest of the members over to the house to play cards. He was the first and only boy Dennis had ever introduced me to. This alone was reason enough for me to think that he must be special. And then, too, I was ready, still scared, but willing to open myself again to the possibility of love.

My first serious relationship had ended only a few months

before I met Herman. I was totally unprepared the day Ronald called and told me he couldn't give me what I needed, that he couldn't love me the way I deserved to be loved. God, I tried to hold on to that man. I called almost every day the first few weeks, I begged, I cried. He was determined though, that he could not, would not love me. But despite the devastation, despite his "inability to love," this relationship taught me more than any other. I always say that I was raised to be a wife and mother, and this, primarily, is what I wanted in my life. But I never knew what to ask, what to expect, what to require from love.

I had watched the women and the men in my family, especially the men—gentle men, drinking men, men working their lives away, doting men, cheating men, men who stayed—and had learned something of what a man's love could offer. But Ronald exposed me to a whole other side of that love. We met in college. He was older than I was by several years and much more experienced and refined. We would go out to breakfast on Sunday mornings and read the papers—the *Chicago Tribune*, the *New York Times*. He would read aloud to me from his favorite sections, business, the arts, and editorials, in that order. Other afternoons, I would make us lunch as he taught me how to play chess. We went to plays, concerts, lectures, and poetry readings.

Through Ronald, I discovered another piece of myself, one which I had always suspected was there, but which had never been nurtured or given the opportunity for expression. As a girl, a daughter, no one had ever before encouraged me to question, to explore the world in the way Ronald did.

I remember the day I knew I truly loved him. It was wintertime, and I had left the house without my gloves. Ronald noticed, and the entire time we were out he held my hands in his to keep them warm.

"Your hands are too beautiful to be cold," he said. The next day, he showed up at my house with a bottle of lotion that was so expensive Mama almost didn't let me keep it, and a new pair of gloves. This is how I discovered what it meant to be loved. I decided that I always wanted to feel like this, to be somebody's center, to be adored and beautiful in someone's eyes. I knew nothing then of choosing, only that I wanted to be chosen.

Meeting Herman that afternoon in my living room brought back all of these feelings, all of the hope that I had shut away when Ronald left. Even though I was twenty-three and he was twenty-four when we met, Herman and I were as tentative and giddy as two high school kids approaching love for the first time. That afternoon alone, I must have changed clothes at least twice, just to impress him. And he was always the one to come back to the kitchen, where I was helping Mama with dinner, to get drinks and snacks for the other guys. After that day, he started to call the house more often for Dennis, and if I answered, we would talk until Dennis pried the phone away.

Soon, he was calling just for me. We started dating regularly. Herman and I both loved music, so we went to every show we could catch. All the big names when they were in town, and then the jazz clubs, where we would huddle close in one of the booths near the stage and he would whisper to me about each musician's sound, how the music made him feel. "It's all up in here," he'd say tapping his chest. I'd get a rush at this display of tenderness, a feeling that welled up and filled my body. I'd want to lose myself then, surrender everything. I was so thrilled just to be near him, his breath warming my cheek, hoping that somewhere inside of him there was room for me along with the music.

When there were no shows we wanted to see, we would spend the weekend with Herman's friends, traveling from party to party. Wherever we went, Herman was always at the center of the good time; his wild antics and laughter, booming across the room over the music, drew everyone in. I enjoyed this side of him as well, especially the way he showed me off to his friends, calling me his "china doll" and "precious."

But my favorite times were when it was just the two of us. We would go to his apartment where he lived with his mother and two sisters. When we had the place to ourselves, he'd play his records as he cooked dinner for us. Later we'd find ourselves entangled on the couch, kissing, touching.

"I never knew anyone like you," he'd whisper, breathless. I was different from the other girls he had dated, more sophisticated, soft-spoken. I came from a good family, I played the piano. He saw all of these things in me. Each new quality he discovered, he unwrapped and regarded as a tiny treasure, a gift that I had given to him.

One evening, Herman's mother walked in on us kissing on the couch. She was furious. "Take her home, Herman! Take her home! I can't believe you would do something like this in my house! In my house!" Herman muttered an apology and hurried me out the door. We drove in silence most of the way to my house.

"We weren't doing anything," I finally said. "We haven't made love. Why is she so upset? Is it that she doesn't like me? I know that's what it is." There. I had said it. All those months of grinning and keeping quiet through Herman's mother's and sisters' snide remarks about me and my family, their not so subtle ways of telling me that I wasn't good enough for their Herman. Part of me was still scared that one day he would look at me and see what his mother saw; that all those things he thought were so special and wonderful would no longer outweigh my many flaws, would no longer be reason enough for him to love me.

"Just tell me, Herman. Your mother hates me, doesn't she?"

"You don't know Mama," he said as we pulled up to my house. He didn't walk me to the door. Not even our usual long kiss goodnight. He barely waited until I was inside before speeding away. I didn't hear from him for two days.

"They're afraid of losing me," was what he told me when he finally called. I agreed to see him that night. We drove down to the lake and sat on the rocks at the water's edge.

"It's been just the four of us for so long," he explained, his voice fading into the waves lapping up against the concrete border. "When my father got sick and moved out of the house, I had to fill the space that he left. I'm the only son. . . . She doesn't hate you . . ." I leaned into him and he let his body go limp against mine.

"I love you," he said. The words hung on the air in a moment of decision, sink or fly. "I don't want to lose you. "Please don't let me lose you."

Two hours before the wedding, I stood in the center of my parents' living room, my wedding dress billowing around my hips. I should feel like floating, I kept thinking to myself. Instead my feet remained glued to the dark green carpet, the rest of my body moving in accordance with the countless pairs of hands, belonging to Mama, my aunts, and cousins, rushing to get me ready for the ceremony.

From across the room, Daddy raised his arm to get my attention and then beckoned, his finger like a hook untangling me from the thick knot of women. He was an island over by the couch, standing rigidly in his rented tux. I went to him, as the women changed shifts—those whose job it was to fix the mess my beautician had made of my hair that morning, giving way to those in charge of my makeup. The dress Mama surprised me and bought last month—I had always thought I would wear the wedding gown I had graduated from high school in—hugged me around the waist, pulling my body into curves. A new body. Didn't seem like mine.

When I reached him, Daddy turned and walked back to the kitchen. I followed. Behind me, I could hear the protests of the women snapping at my heels. "Marlene, there's no time for this! You got to finish getting ready!" And then Mama's voice, holding them off, making space for me, like always. "Give her a minute with her daddy. She won't be long."

The kitchen, usually the busiest room in the house, was empty. The radio, tuned to the news station, which Mama turned on first thing every morning after she got up, was still on. The table was cluttered with the remains of that morning's breakfast, which no one had had the time or the energy to clear away. Daddy turned the radio off and pushed aside the dishes so that I could sit down. Once I was settled in my chair, he took his place at the head of the table. I watched as he laid his palms flat, fingers outstretched, his thumbs curled around underneath the table to grip the edge.

When I was younger, looking at my father's hands like this, it seemed that his thumbs were the only things anchoring him, were what kept him there at the dinner table with us, as though if he were to let go he would just float away. I sensed the tenuous balance Daddy had managed to create, a momentary stability between the forces in his life that at once nurtured and opposed one another.

*Mama had called us in earlier than usual that Saturday, during the best part of the day, when the sun was still climbing and plans were being made. That cool hour before noon, before heat was a weight on our skin, when I could jump rope with my sweater on and my ends wouldn't turn, when even the knees of Dennis's pants were clean.*

*"Marlene! Dennis! Time to come inside!" Mama's voice caught me in midair, just when I had made peace (once again) with my feet, two sizes bigger than the other girls'; just when I had perfected an understanding of gravity and had slid into a groove with the rhythm my feet, the clothesline rope, and concrete made; just when I was about to reach that place where mine would be the story passed up and down the block, two and three times; just when I was becoming beautiful . . .*

*"Marlene! Dennis! I said time to come inside!"*

*"It's not lunchtime. It's not time for our bath," Dennis and I protested, dragging our feet as we followed Mama down the hall to our apartment.*

*"I know what time it is," Mama snapped.*

*"Then why do we have to come inside?" Dennis whined.*

*"We have somewhere to go," Mama answered, jingling the apartment keys in her pocket. It seemed a pretty fair trade, coming inside early for the possibility of adventure. After all, "somewhere to go" wasn't like saying we were going to the store or over to Aunt Agnes's, which we usually did on Saturdays. Somewhere could be a place we'd never been before.*

*Mama insisted that we change clothes, even though we had hardly been outside long enough to get dirty. Thankfully, she didn't make us take a bath. Instead, she filled the bathroom sink with soapy water and made each of us scrub with a facecloth. When we were clean enough to dress, Mama told us to wear something not quite Sunday, but not like everyday. I chose my lemon-yellow dress and the patent leather shoes Daddy had bought for me two Easters ago.*

*Mama was locking the front door behind us before either Dennis or I thought to ask where we were going.*

*"To see your Daddy."* My heart sank. *All this just to go see Daddy? Just to walk over to the gas station?*

*"Come on,"* Mama said and reached back for our hands, pulling us up to match her pace.

Daddy was in front of the station waiting as we walked up. He had changed out of the coveralls he wore as his uniform into the shirt and pants Mama had ironed for him that morning. He waved excitedly when he saw us and rushed toward us.

*"Come on! Come on!"* he said, leading me and Dennis to a small office next to the garage part of the station.

*"See, this is where I sit."* Daddy pointed to a desk cluttered with papers, each one stamped with the name of the station and its blue and white emblem. A plain calendar, with the year 1953 in red across the top, was the only decoration on the white cinderblock wall in front of the desk.

*"I can look out this window here and see everything going on outside,"* Daddy gestured proudly. I looked out of the window that took up most of the wall. All I could see was cars pulling in and out of the station, attendants leaning lazily against the gas pumps as they filled their tanks. But I nodded back at Daddy, for I had the feeling that he really wanted me to see something more than that.

*"I want you all to meet some people,"* Daddy said. We followed him outside, over near the pumps, where he introduced us to four black men congregated there. *"This is my family,"* he said, gathering us around him. *"This is my son, Dennis; my daughter, my oldest, Marlene; and my wife, Anna."* I liked the way the men reached out and shook my hand. I liked it when they called me princess, when they said I looked just like Mama, and then said I was going to be tall like Daddy.

*"Well, we're gonna get a move on,"* Daddy said, pulling away from the men. *"Mr.———— know I'm gone."* He looked over at the white man standing in the doorway of the garage and waved.

"*Anybody hungry?*" *Daddy asked as we walked down the street toward the Walgreens drugstore on the corner. When Dennis and I saw where we were going, it was all we could do not to take off running ahead of Mama and Daddy. None of our friends had ever been to Walgreens to sit down and eat. We had never been before now. Whenever we went into the store with Mama, we always drifted towards the lunch counter to get a whiff of the hamburgers, the thin, perfect circles—not like Mama's hamburgers which looked like fists in the skillet—laid out on the grill in neat little rows, in varying shades of pink and brown. "We have food at home," Mama would say when she found us.*

*But being here now, sitting in one of the booths, the plastic seat sticking to my legs, was like the time Mama let me take the bus by myself to Auntie's hotel, or when she had decided I was old enough to walk to school with my friends. I felt grown-up, important.*

*Dennis and I ordered hamburgers. Daddy and Mama both had fried chicken-in-a-basket. After the waitress left our table, Daddy pulled out a small, wax-paper envelope. Inside was an oval shaped patch like the one he already had on his uniform, the same blue and white as the gas station logo, except in the middle was his name, not the station's, and on this new patch, two other words:* ASSISTANT MANAGER, *in gold cursive lettering beneath the bold* JACK DUDLEY *in blue.*

"*It's official,*" *Daddy said, handing the patch to Mama.*

"*I thought you were going to have them put 'Harrison' instead of 'Jack' on it this time. That's your proper name.*"

"*Too many letters. Besides, everybody knows me as Jack. Nobody but Daddy calls me Harrison, and that's only sometime.*"

"*Honey, I think it's wonderful,*" *Mama beamed. "I'll sew it on tonight.*"

"*Another thing,*" *Daddy took a long drag from his pop. "I hear Mr.——— is thinking about selling the place. He said his wife wants to move out to one of the new developments in the suburbs. I think he just wants to get away from all these colored folks, you know? He's made some good money off of that place, couldn't be any other reason. Anyway, Al and I have been talking about going into business together, and I was thinking we could try and buy the station."*

*"But Jack, you just made assistant manager. Why don't you give yourself time to get a feel for the business before you jump into something?"*

*"Thing is, if we can do it, we got to act now."*

*"Where is your brother going to get the money to buy a filling station? How do you plan to come up with it, for that matter?"*

*"I don't know yet. We have to think about it."*

*"It's a good idea, honey," Mama softened her voice. "I just want us to have everything together before we jump into something as big as that. I thought we had agreed buying a house would be our next big purchase . . ."*

*"I want to make it so we can do both," Daddy said. "Anyway, it's just something I'm thinking about." The words subsided into the quiet which spread over the table. I noticed Daddy's hands for the first time that day, spread wide and anchored by his thumbs hooked beneath the table. I thought about the science experiment we had done in school that week. My teacher was trying to explain magnetic attraction and had given each of us a pair of rectangular magnets. I remembered the loud click the magnets had made as the oppositely charged ends were drawn together, and the refusal of the two like ends to meet, even when I tried to force them. It occurred to me that Daddy inhabited this place of suspension, between two powerful forces kept apart by the strength of their resistance . . .*

I had wanted to tell him that day, as I wanted to tell him now, especially now, that I understood. I knew this feeling of being caught between two worlds, not being able to let either one go.

"I wish I could do more." Daddy. Apologizing again when there was nothing to apologize for. *He hears the sound of blood pulsing. Eyes straining toward something never seen. This constant hum. . . . He struggles for a way to reconcile the dream and the work. The work that doesn't end in the realization of the dream, but with itself.* "I had hoped to give you all something to put down on a house," he said, looking away.

*When would it ever be enough?*

All the time he spent working, I spent wanting to be special enough, good enough for him. I remembered all the wonderful things he had done for me as a child, the Christmas he went and searched every toy and department store there was until he found the Patty Jo doll, the first black doll, I had begged for; chauffeuring me and my girlfriends around to every party, dance, and movie we wanted to attend. But even so, I wasn't sure that he loved me. I wanted him to hug me, laugh and joke around with me the way he did with my cousins and the girls Dennis brought home. He always seemed to think they were so pretty, so special. I looked at his hands again, the white of his knuckles showing through the deep reddish-brown blanket of skin; his thick fingers, with their loose pockets of skin wrinkling in the center, the way I imagined Mama's belly had rumpled and folded, empty of children.

"Daddy, what you gave was enough," I told him, finally. "All I ever wanted was for you to love me; to know that you loved me, for you to say it."

On the way to the church, Daddy and I huddled close in the back seat of the car. "I can't believe this is happening," he sighed. I knew what he meant. I felt as though I were watching all of this on television, my life flashing across a screen.

Uncle Lipsey, Aunt Agnes's husband, driving us in his Lincoln Towncar, took the same route that we traveled every Sunday from the house we had purchased on Drexel Avenue in 1956, eight years ago, back to the old neighborhood, to Corpus Christi, the church we attended when we were living in the apartment on 49th and Vincennes.

Down Cottage Grove, through Washington Park— where Daddy used to take us canoeing, and where we had our picnics and went bike riding—to 51st and South Parkway, continuing down to 49th Street, one of many routes taken by people like us. I saw myself everywhere: a girl waving at me from the bank of the pond in the park; her face smiling in the windows of stores where Mama and I used to shop; the bangs, turned under that morning, blowing back from her forehead as she walked with her group of friends against the wind.

We had invited close to seven hundred people to the wedding: Family from all over the country. Memphis, Warrior, New Orleans, St. Louis, Detroit, some from as far away as Los Angeles. Friends from our old neighborhoods, people Herman and I had grown up with, gone to grammar school, high school, and college with. Colleagues from work, as well as those in the expansive, though tightly knit group we had come to belong to as a couple, whose parties we attended regularly and with whom we ran the streets to dances and concerts on the weekends.

As we neared the church, I began to see these familiar faces, walking towards the already thick swarm of people milling around on the church steps and spilling into the street, each one its own screen, displaying some scene, some piece of the story of the life that had brought me here, to this day. We pulled up to the side entrance where it was less crowded. Uncle Lipsey got out and opened my door. *I'm not ready,* I wanted to say to Daddy, but the bridesmaids, incandescent in their salmon colored gowns, had already surrounded me, and were now steering me into the church.

When I saw him waiting for me at the altar, Herman, tall and lanky, handsome in his tuxedo, I fell in love all over again. And I saw how much he loved me. I knew it was right. I clutched Daddy's arm tightly as we walked down the aisle. Herman reached for my hand and held it firmly, but my other arm was still entwined with Daddy's. I turned to look back at Mama, at the family and friends who filled the pews of the church, just as they had when I was christened at this same altar as a baby, when I received my first Holy Communion, graduated from grammar school, when I was crowned queen of the Pastor's Tea. Only then, when I saw that they were all still there, would be there even after I turned around and stepped into the life that was waiting for me with Herman, was I able to let Daddy's arm go.

*He lay on his back next to me. I cuddled up to him and stretched my legs across his stomach. He moved his arms from behind his head, encircling and pulling me closer. His hands, caressing gently, explored the length of my body. Words of a song found the rhythm of his movements,* you touched me. *Nothing else matters when you're near me, I thought to myself. I hate it when you're away. Your smell lingers with me. I feel the places where you've been and ache for the fullness you bring. Why can't it always be like this?*

A year into our marriage, I spent my days pacing the cramped apartment his mother insisted we take, waiting for him to come home from work or an evening out with his friends. His mother and sister, in the apartment one floor down from ours, would call for him on the hour, barely even saying hello when I answered the phone. I cooked, cleaned, prepared for the moment when he would walk through our door and back into my arms. But the home I tried to create never seemed to be enough. I was always in competition with his friends and family, his drinking, all of which he was unwilling to give up. Why was it always this way with us, each of us pulling in different directions, unable to find the compromise, the balance, and unable to let go?

> I . . . I'm so in love with you,
> whatever you want to do, is alright with me . . .

I remember the night of my first miscarriage. We had been trying for five years to have children, although the doctors had told us that the likelihood was small. Something inside of me had been damaged in the accident I was in when I was eighteen, when I almost lost my life. But what do doctors know? They told my family I'd never wake from the coma I was in. And when I opened my eyes three weeks later, they told me I'd never walk again, yet I left the hospital on my own two feet. I have always sensed this possibility in myself, this power, even, to go beyond the places most people are willing to stop. But when they said I couldn't have children, I began to doubt this power, to question my body. Maybe the strength was all gone, and inside I had become like an old clay pot left out in the hot sun, dried and cracked, no longer able to hold anything.

Still, I prayed for my babies, and at the end of our fifth year of marriage I got pregnant. I was four months along that night. Herman and I were throwing a dinner party. I wasn't feeling well and suggested that we postpone the party until next weekend, but Herman really had his heart set on having it.

"How are we going to let everybody know on such short

notice? Besides, it's been a long time since all of us have been together," he reasoned. I convinced myself that I would be fine once all the preparations were finished. I spent the entire afternoon cooking for the twenty or so guests we had invited. By the time everyone arrived, I was exhausted and feeling worse than I had earlier. I told Herman that I was going to take a nap, and he gave me a quick kiss on the cheek, his breath laced with alcohol.

"Call me if you need me," he said and turned back to his friends before I could respond. This is how he gets at parties, I reminded myself. He's just having a good time. I heard his laugh rising above the din of music and conversation. But as I walked to the bedroom, I couldn't shake the feeling that if I turned around everyone would be pointing and staring at me, the laugh I had always loved for the way it encircled a room, pulling everybody into its embrace, now directed at me.

let me be the one you come running to . . .

Somebody was stabbing me. A man hovering over the bed plunging a knife into my stomach. "Wait. Please wait. I'm pregnant. You're going to hurt my baby. Not my baby," I muttered in my sleep, unable to scream. When I opened my eyes, there was no man, no knife. For a moment I was relieved, but then the stabbing began again. Sounds from the party outside seeped into the bedroom: the stinging slap of cards against the tabletop, conversation rising and falling in waves over my head, bass notes matching the rapid throbbing in my stomach.

I'll never be untrue . . .

I felt the first drops of blood trickle onto the sheets. I raised my legs and pressed my knees together to hold it back, the way the doctors had taught me. The blood kept coming stronger, I couldn't stop it. *God, no.* "Herman," I called. I felt as though I was screaming, but the sound had barely pierced the darkness. It seemed like hours before he heard me and came into the room. He sat down on the edge of the bed.

"I'm losing the baby," I told him. He let out a long, deep sigh but said nothing.

"Sonny! Come on man, it's your play!" a voice from the living room called.

"Everything's going to be alright," he said, rising from the bed. "I'll be back as soon as I finish this hand."

I lay there soaked in my tears and blood, unable to move. When Herman returned, I told him to call the doctor. He turned on the light and I closed my eyes, not wanting to see the blood, not wanting to believe any of this had happened. Herman left to pick up the medicine the doctor had prescribed. He brought me a glass of water and a pill when he got home, then went back to his card game. The hollow in my stomach, the loss I felt, engulfed the room. I lay there suspended, alone as I had never been in all my life, alone as I would be time and time again.

This night uncovered a gap between us that we would never repair, even after the babies, the four who stayed, were born. It was only during the three months before Herman's death, the happiest time in our marriage, that we were able to forgive and love each other fully. How is it that love surfaces so clearly, so perfectly, when there is nothing left to lose?

When we arrive at the hospital, the doctor tells me that Mama's condition has not improved, and that I will have to wait until the nurses finish giving her a bath before I can see her. I decide to call the kids to let them know I made it in. I call my son, Omar, in Atlanta first, and tell him what's going on and where I am. When he asks if he should try to get to Chicago, I tell him I don't know.

"Just stay close by. Be ready," I say. He presses for more information.

"But how's Nana? What are the doctors saying?" I know he needs reassurance, a promise that everything is going to be okay. But it is more than I can give.

"Look honey, I don't want to talk too much right now. I'll call you later. Love you, baby." I gently press the lever between the two hooks where the mouthpiece rests to disconnect the call. It is as though I have placed my fingers over his lips, the way I used to when he was younger, our signal for quiet time, a soft click silencing the urgency of his voice.

I pick up the receiver again and hold it, listening to the drone of the dial tone vibrating in my ear. *Do it*, it seemed to say. *Dial the number.* I have to call my oldest daughter, Tasha, in DC, but I'm not ready, not yet. The numbers on the key pad are a blur whenever I lift my finger to touch them. How would she take this news? She and Mama had gotten so close over the past couple years. And then she would be worried about me. Who would be there for her? Who could she call? She didn't have anybody in DC but that simple ass she was dating, who had moved everything but his furniture into her apartment and wasn't paying for shit! He was probably asleep by now. Won't give up his precious sleep for anything . . .

I knew that my other kids would be upset when I told them about Mama, but I also knew that they would ultimately be okay. Somehow they had learned to shield themselves on the inside, to feel the hurt and then let it go. But Tasha, she absorbs it, holds on. There are times when she sinks into a funk, when I can look into her face and see the pain clouding her eyes but don't know where it started or how to get it to end.

When she was a baby, she would wake up every day smiling, the happiest child I have ever seen.

But something happened somewhere, something I didn't see, something I couldn't protect her from. Now she takes everything in on herself and won't let go. If some worthless boy doesn't like her or won't treat her right, it's because she isn't pretty enough; or if something else doesn't happen the way she'd hoped, it's because she's not smart enough, not good enough.

Even when she doesn't say it, I hear her thinking it, the constant whir of questions. I know this, because sometimes it feels as though we share the same skin; we are that close. I know this, because she is like I was at her age, the same outward looking eyes, searching for her own reflection in somebody else's face; the same heart-stabbing yearning, the ache for fulfillment. I know this, because I am her mother and I have spent my life trying to save her from this hunger, this pain, the way my mother saved me.

As I hang up the phone, having reached my youngest daughter, Elizabeth, the last of my children, the doctor signals to let me know that I can go in to see Mama. I walk slowly down the corridor, traveling a lifetime in just those few steps. As I enter the room, I call out the first words I speak whenever I return, "Mama, I'm home."

# 3

# NATASHA

*Evolution of Love*

# I

One night, a little girl appeared in my dreams. She was clutching a bundle of shiny stones to her chest. Encased in these stones were my stories, those I had forgotten, those I chose not to remember, those I didn't know. She turned to face me before tossing the stones into the air. They fell around her in a shower of multicolored flowers. As she began to collect them, she beckoned for me to join her, but I was unable to move.

When I awakened, I realized that the little girl in my dream was me, her image taken from a photograph of myself when I was four or five years old. I wore a pink and white party dress, my hair pulled up into a bun on top of my head. I was always drawn to this picture because of the blank expression on my face. The eyes, staring almost defiantly, seemed to ask nothing from the world, but at the same time begged for definition, meaning. Whenever I look into those eyes it feels as though I'm looking into a mirror.

The little girl returned the next night. This time she stood at the edge of a dark place, looking at me, with that blank face. She was waiting for me to follow her into the darkness. "I'm not ready," I said. The little girl disappeared.

## II

April 1994

Mom,

The boys may run wild as greens, but for us, daughters, leaving home is still the most difficult thing. We daughters grow up clothed in the skin of women—mother, grandmothers, aunts—their scents, their rhythms. Sometimes it can feel like you share the same heart. Which is why it is such a surprise when you begin to hear a second faint—at first—pounding beneath the louder pulsing you've grown accustomed to. You recognize this small sound as your own heartbeat. And sometimes you pretend you don't hear it so that you don't have to leave the warmth and the security of home, the warmth and the security that the women hope will sustain you, so that you will never leave them.

Which is why it hurts so much when the faint pounding becomes a roar that you can no longer ignore, that you must follow; why the women feel as though something has been physically torn away from them when you finally decide to go. Why our own leaving haunts us.

Night bleeds to daylight; the struggle of a black sky to remain black, begun and always lost, when the last barely blue sigh gives way to a light that pulls back all of the covers, gets into the quiet, sealed-off places and breaks them open.

For us, this day always comes. It is as inevitable as the sun overtaking the moon, interrupting the com-

fortable and familiar space we carefully managed to
create again during this short visit. I awaken at this
moment, covered in the pale light of early morning,
my head heavy with the knowledge that today, as I
have done now many times since my freshman year
of college, I am leaving home.

I heave myself out of bed when I hear your alarm
go off, wading through the air, now thick with layers
of guilt and sadness accumulated over this night, and
the many nights I've spent dreading this morning.
The sun pokes me with its sharp pointed fingers.
Time to get up. Time to get moving.

I hear you rising, slowly. Neither of us has had any
sleep, and we fight to keep our eyes open as we stum-
ble through the familiar routine. We move around
the house in the half-light like shadows, vulnerable
flames flickering against the wall. We don't speak,
avoid one another's eyes, keeping busy with small details, trying our best to shield ourselves from words. I
double-check the suitcase, which has been sitting by
the door since last night, its looming presence never
letting us forget the departure that lies ahead.

I am tempted to say, to think, that we have grown
accustomed to these mornings. But I know "accustomed" is the wrong word. I don't believe anyone
can become accustomed to pain. As much as we're
used to it. As much as it's expected. Our black lives
are living testimony to this. We walk on tenuous
ground, still, never assured of our safety when we
leave our homes or even inside of them; never knowing from whose lips the unutterable will be uttered;
whose fist will strike the first blow.

I write to you now, from my seat on this slow-

moving train, what I could not say when we were
face to face. I look out the window to wave one last
time, catching a glimpse of your face already wet
with tears. I am thankful for the silence the window
puts between us.

We have just lurched forward, the wheels gaining
momentum, taking me further away from home. I
watch the familiar place marks of the city fall behind,
until the landscape becomes foreign, a series of trees
and houses, names I don't recognize. I, like this train,
am a fleeting presence, a small break in the circle of
air, of breath, surrounding a place, which mends itself and closes as soon as we have passed through,
as if we were never there.

I always thought I would be the one who stayed.
I've never been one to wander for the sake of wandering. So it isn't that I begin this journey in search of another place. I have long since stopped loving cities,
relying on a place to make me a home. When we first
left Chicago and moved to Boston, with its frigid
buildings and inhabitants, I realized that cities could
(and did) change like seasons.

What lurches us forward into motion and what
sustains us?

I learned to put my faith in the living, marking my
travels by the people rather than the place. They, and
the potential for them, are what draws and keeps me.
And home is the feeling we create for one another,
and carry with us wherever we are. With this in mind
and in heart, I begin my own journey, a search not
only for who I am to become, but also for who I have
been.

Many have walked before me and are walking
beside me even now. I am convinced that history is a

cycle of movement and rest and we, the ones of here and now, keep it going. The dreams that burned in the hearts of our folks long ago, the words they folded up and carried beneath their tongues—*freedom equality belonging comfort safety*—are passed on to us, recycled into a language we can understand.

The wheels beneath me rolling, tell me, *don't look back*; urge me to keep my eyes forward, fixed only on what they can see ahead, on what is certain, immediately knowable. *Don't look back,* they plead. The past is full of questions, some unanswerable. *Don't look back.* But I always do.

## III

*Could they see my arrival as they prayed, worked, made love, fought for, dreamed about, ran away to a place where I could be born in relative safety and carrying their name? Where my back would remain smooth, albeit my heart might be bruised and my spine would still be prone to curving over? Did they see my reflection in the black water of swamps and lagoons shimmering under the moonlight, beneath the soles of their feet as they crossed, or staring up at them from the dirty water of other people's filth? Did they hear my voice in the din and hiss of smoke-spitting, blood-devouring machines and factories? Was it my heartbeat they heard beneath the bass line that drove the drums, like dogs snapping at the heels of a man running for his life, running to his life?*

## IV

The night before I was born, my father cooked a big dinner for my mother. Salisbury steak and mashed potatoes with gravy. My parents had invited one of my father's friends over, a man named Fred who always claimed to be my mother's "second husband," and who my two sisters, my brother, and I remember as the man who called us "little niggers" whenever we saw him.

"Aw, man, that don't mean nothing," he'd protest whenever our parents would say something to him about it. Nigger was not a word we used in our house, but my sisters and brother and I cried laughing, thrilled to no end when Fred said it. We would sneak away from the adults to another room to try it out for ourselves. "Hey, little nigger," we'd whisper to one another, breaking into hysterics before we could even get the word out. It was bad, jarring, against the soft cooing sounds we heard and which defined us in our own house— poo poo, honey, pumpkin, baby. Nigger was like the shiny silver pistol my father kept in the cabinet above the stove, loaded and dangerous. Just whispering it made us feel closer to something our parents wouldn't condone, something they couldn't control.

But that was much later. Before we started to yearn for the grit, the saltiness, the danger of something else, there was only our parents' hope and the protective world they created from this hope for us to enter. There was this night, before I was born, when my mother sat in the living room of my parent's two-bedroom apartment—right above the apartment where my grandmother and my aunt, my father's mother and sister, lived—watching my father and Fred prepare this wonderful meal just for her, enjoying being waited on. "Hand and foot," my mother says, still beaming whenever she tells this story. "Your Daddy really wanted to make that night special."

There is another story Mom tells, though not as often. The story of the miscarriage she had during a party she and Daddy were giving; how my father finally came after what seemed like hours of her calling from the dark bedroom, and stayed only after the last hand of cards had been played. I suspect this is where my story really begins, with my mother's prayers and desire, her tears and her loneliness. There were others, before me, who passed through my mother's womb in a river of blood and water. I was the first one who stayed.

Mom went into labor around nine o'clock the morning I was born. She and Daddy had arrived at the hospital at least an hour earlier, but the people at the front kept asking for information. "Look, you already have our insurance papers. Just get my wife up to the goddamn room!" Daddy, raising his voice, running back and forth between the check-in desk and Mom lying on a stretcher panting in short quick breaths like her mother taught her.

Finally, they brought Mom upstairs. "We thought for sure you were ready to be born, the way you were coming down when we were checking in," she says smiling. "But as soon as we got to the room, you changed your mind and went right back up. You were determined to come into the world on your own terms." Mom lay there for hours while I decided when I would be born. She talked to me the way she had since my conception. *We are disappointed queens, me on this table, you inside me. The world is not all that we hoped, but there are good things and space for breathing . . .*

I was born that night, January 6, 1971, at 9:51 P.M.

"You were so beautiful," Mom gushes. "This precious little red baby with steel gray eyes and a head full of jet black hair. They let me hold you, and I felt like I knew you already, all those conversations we had had when you were in my tummy. And then your daddy held you. He was so proud of his baby girl. . . . God, he loved you." Outside of the room, my grandparents, aunts, uncles, and several family friends had assembled. "Everybody was waiting for you to be born."

My parents brought me home a couple days later, their apartment packed with friends and relatives who had come to meet "Herman and Marlene's baby girl." The firstborn. Mom set out a tub in the middle of the living room, and the women proceeded to give me a bath, anointing me in their sounds, their scent, claiming me as their own.

I have witnessed the song and dance of men and women coming together and separating, joining again; an elaborate ritual of tentative steps and pauses, lunges and retreats. I have heard the voices of women turn milky and watched them strip layers of their days' work to curves fundamental as bone. I have watched the women sparkle, laugh, content in their own skins, blessing their images before mirrors rising like domes from lace-covered bureaus. And I have seen the men arrive, sweet-smelling of cologne and cigars, hats in hand, shoes shiny as stars. I have watched them remove some of the weight they wear in the world and become light, their voices riding the wind like autumn leaves. I have seen hearts unwrapped from brown paper skins. I was christened in their rhythm. The women named me beauty, and the men all called me baby.

V

hands
watch them    you've seen them before    they are the same
      hands you reach for to cross the busy streets    hands
      which draw out fever    hands connected to the body
      to the mouth    which tells you you are perfect
      *mom?*
      *yes, baby?*
      *nothin'*

watch these hands spread a piece of old newspaper on the
    countertop by the stove     watch these hands become
    the sturdy hands of a surgeon laying out his
    instruments:     a jar of blue ultra sheen     the hot comb
    and the wide-mouthed curling iron     once a shiny
    copper you could see yourself in     not really your
    reflection     but some figment of yourself stretched
    into oblong shapes and colors     now two black eyes
    closed against these years of burning
    your face     a charred memory

remember     the first time you found out about the hot
    comb     when mom asked daddy to pick one up at the
    store     except you thought she had asked for a hot
    *cone*     so all the while daddy is gone     and you and
    mom are taking turns singing along with your favorite
    record     *feelings     nothing more than feelings* and
    you're singing extra hard when it gets to your part
    you're getting yourself all set to taste mom's hot
    *cone*     which you're thinking is some new kind of ice
    cream     and you're even a little mad that mom didn't
    tell daddy to bring one back for you
    *alright honey, im ready.     drag that chair over here by the*
    *stove and sit down*

tickticktickticktickticktick     gas catching     your heart
    racing     fire blossoms before your eyes     so pretty
    close up     a wild blue flower     you just want to
    hold     just want to touch     *ah uh! you know better than*
    *to play with fire!* keep watching the flames     stare
    straight into the flickering heart until you see yourself
    there     you learn how to talk with fire     to draw the
    cool out of these hot hot blues     it's like being
    swallowed by the sky     or melting     dancing like this

*that night    i surrendered to the flames*
*a walk through fire to the promised place*
*of beauty    but there are still questions like*
*where was i before i crossed over?*

order out of chaos    god created earth from a ball of mud
and human beings rose up from the dust    mom parts
your hair into squares    runs a finger tipped with blue
ultra sheen along the lines of your scalp    then she is
rubbing it all over your head    you imagine your hair
is as blue as the water in the ymca pool

you are surrounded    by the smell of your own hair
burning another layer of black on the hot comb    this
is the smell of granny on a saturday    your best friend
leaning over to tell you a secret    the shiny kneed
girls who rule the playground    now it belongs
to you

you like the warmth of this new hair pressed against your
ear    its flatness its slipperiness    you like that the
comb goes right through it    and that it moves
without you even trying    but there are questions like
how long can i keep it? is it really mine?

*don't get up from here and start running stop touching it*
*you'll take the style out and please let me braid it before*
*you get in the tub you can't let any water splash on your*
*hair*

how having walked through fire    you still look back
and wonder.

## VI

*The skin of children, hugging tightly rib cages and collarbones, rounding to elbows and knees, secures them in their notions of speed, of agelessness, of flight. We will always run this way, hitting and breaking the wind with our fists. And we will always be smooth, our faces do not crumble, our spines will never bend us toward the ground. Someday we will grow wings from our arms and shoulders, someday when we are angels.*

Summer dusk paled to dark. Our upturned faces watched the sun, a faded pink Red Hot someone sucked all the sticky crimson heat off of, descend on us like a blessing. Those nights, Mom and Daddy let us stay out even after the sky had called in all of its colors; had turned itself the deep purple of windows like the closed eyes of a sleeping house.

We preyed on a different light: the yellowish green or white sparks of lightning bugs. Waited breathless for the first sudden twinkle that signified the beginning of the chase. With one hand clasping an empty pickle jar, the other fishing the air, we ran after the lightning bugs' sporadic flickering. Those nights, nothing seemed beyond our reach. Life was just another thing to hold in our sweaty palms, to collect in empty jars and containers with lids screwed on so tightly not even air could escape.

In the afternoon after school, two or three times a week, my sister and brother and I made the trek from our house up to the Texaco station to replenish our candy supply. For some reason, the Texaco station was the only place our parents would let us walk without them, although it was just as far away—three or four long blocks—as any place else we might have imagined walking, *and* we had to cross a busy street to get there. We didn't argue the point.

At the Texaco, we made our selections from rows of clear plastic and glass containers full of penny and five-cent candies—PAL penny gum, Now and Laters (pronounced Nowlaters or Nowalaters), Lemonheads and wine candy, also known as Jolly Ranchers—lining the shelves behind a thick sheet of foggy bulletproof glass, which ran the length of the counter.

There was no glass when we first started coming here. We could rest our hands on the counter and watch the man count out our purchases, even reach into one of the containers ourselves if we got bold. There was a "mini-mart," one of the first combo gas station/convenience stores in our area, that you could walk around in. Mom or Daddy sometimes sent us there to buy something they needed for that night's dinner, or an item they had forgotten to get in the "real" store. You could squeeze the loaves of bread and choose the softest; hold cans of pop from the cooler against your cheek to find the coldest.

That was in the late seventies, soon after my youngest sister was born and my parents sold our house on 91st and Michigan to buy the two-flat building on 68th and Chappel. By 1981, the entire area behind the counter had been sealed off by an impenetrable wall of glass. We crowded into the narrow rectangular area between the counter and the entrance, joining the single-file line, snaking all the way to the rear wall and then doubling back on itself, of people waiting to place gas and cigarette orders at the window up front.

The door leading to the mini-mart had been soldered shut, although the market was still open. The cashier would yell out whatever it was you wanted, and someone else behind the counter would run into the mini-mart area to get it. If what you bought was too big to fit through the revolving window at the register, someone would bring it around for you. You could no longer touch the thing you wanted until you paid for it, and, even then, you had to take whatever they gave you.

To get to the Texaco station, we took the back way, through the alley, pushing into the territory of the big boys. Boys who were rumored to belong to the much feared (and revered) Disciples gang, stories of whose escapades permeated our insulated neighborhood of middle-class black families. Boys who slithered into our yard, past our fence, past my parents' hopes that private schools, a relatively stable family, and money would be enough to keep them out.

They came to steal the sour green apples that grew on the tree in our backyard and, once, all of our bikes from our basement. Big boys you couldn't help but love for their badness, the rudeness of their walk. Big boys, bad boys, invincible, infinite, despite our best weapons against them. One time, we concocted a poison in our garage— made from paint, mud, glue, water, and worms—and injected it into apples strategically placed in the crux of the tree's thick limbs and on the windowsill of the garage facing the alley. None of the big boys ever took the bait.

When the poisoned apples didn't work, our next line of defense was our parents. Once Mom actually spanked one of the boys who had come into the yard and called her a bitch when she asked him to leave. This was a time before bullets would be fired quicker than words, a time when adults didn't fear children as enemies. After the spanking, Mom invited the boy, who was around eleven or twelve, to come over and play in the yard sometime. He seemed to consider the invitation for a moment, standing there, scrawny, snot-nosed and puffy-eyed, at the edge of our yard. But his eyes rapidly glazed over, his lips curling into a defiant sneer, as he mumbled something about coming back to kick all of our asses, before turning and stepping back into the alley.

I saw a big boy cry that day; the way he didn't run away when Mom released him, how his gaze lingered. I remember his face when I see the faces of other big boys flashing across the screen on the evening news, flickering past me on the street. And I wonder if maybe their eyes aren't really the stones everyone says they are, but more like eggshells, a yolk of uncried tears swimming around inside.

Those Texaco afternoons, walking through the alley gave us some of the big boys' badness—before we discovered our own. It was the place where we tested speed and boundaries, leaning against the one thing certain in our lives: We were always close to home.

One afternoon, after we had made the trek and were sitting on the sun-warmed sidewalk in front of our house, counting and separating our candy into small mounds on our laps, our friend Darryl—whom we called Egghead Darryl, because of the pronounced oval shape of his head—walked up to the fringes of our circle to give us some news. Darryl lived across the alley with his grandfather in the three-flat building behind our house. He had come to report that there had been three murders in the apartment above his last night.

"Y'all seen the news today?" he asked us, arms crossed, chest puffed out slightly with the importance of his story. We shook our heads, no. A whole family had been "wiped out," he said matter-of-factly, stabbed to death while they slept. We knew them. We saw the mother, a black woman, and the father, a white minister, all the time cleaning behind their building, unpacking groceries from their car, calling for their kids. We had played with the children, a girl named Rhonda, who was around my age, nine or ten, and her brother, Steven, who couldn't have been more than five. They weren't part of the group of kids we hung out with from the neighborhood. They almost never played piggy or running bases with us in our driveway. They never rode their bikes up and down the block. But we knew them.

As Darryl told it, the father's son from a previous marriage, who was white and crazy, hated his father for marrying a black woman. So he broke into their apartment and stabbed everybody inside. Rhonda, who was away at camp, was the only one who survived. Imagine going away for a week and coming home to find your entire family gone, never coming back. Imagine being the only one left.

After that day, we didn't walk up to the Texaco nearly as often. And when death boldly stepped out of the alley and entered our house, taking our father two summers later, we stopped going altogether. We went inside, most days before the sun had set all the way. Nobody waited for dark. We watched the lightning bugs sometimes, as they shimmered up to our windows. But too soon, even that light dimmed and faded away. We turned instead to the steady blue stream emanating from the television, the light that could survive encased in glass, the faces we knew would still be there smiling and alive the next morning.

## VII

There are nights when our house threatens to fall down at the sound of his key jiggling the front door lock. Daddy is a policeman and works the late-night shift. He sleeps during the day and doesn't come home sometimes until two or three o'clock in the morning. I lie awake beneath my covers and the soft sleeping sounds my brother and sisters make. I am waiting for him; eyes stretched wide against exhaustion, listening for our blue Chevy Nova to growl up the driveway.

As soon as I hear the last cough of the engine, I slip out of bed and position myself behind the wall in the hallway so that I can get a clear look at him when he comes through the door. I hold my breath and wait for the moment when he steps inside; wait to see how much he'll falter, or if the smell of liquor will rise off of him like steam. I wait to hear Mom getting up, the creak from her and Daddy's half-empty bed, the whisper of her slippered feet padding toward him in long strides down the hallway.

I have learned how to turn concave, like an upside-down umbrella; to empty myself in order to catch the words, zig-zagging and exploding, shredding the small circle of air between my parents' lips, and swallow. I have learned to see through these nights to stillness and to lean against my goodness, my wide-open eyes, hoping they will be enough to get us to morning.

*We were standing in the kitchen one night . . . you were swaying like a tree just broken at the knees, deciding which way to fall . . . you promised . . . remember you said, I'm not gonna do it anymore, pumpkin. I'ma stop all this, stop coming home like this . . . you promised . . .*

In the eye of a storm, there is so much you can't see: the tops of trees waving, a cry, a plea for the Spirit, holy places. A song hidden in the wind. Mom knows the song. This is why she stays, why she keeps screaming and crying after Daddy on these nights when he has already turned and walked away; when I pull on the sleeve of her robe, or call her from my bed if they make me go back to my room, begging her to run away, escape. All I see is rage, and I try to make my body into a wall that can protect her from it. But she is fighting for the song she knows is turning somewhere in Daddy's heart, the

one they had begun to sing together what seems like a lifetime ago. Mom says, *it wasn't always like this.* I don't believe
her. I have only ever seen my parents kiss once.

*Your daddy used to call me precious. Did you know that? All
his friends knew me by that name, and they would come by the
house telling me how Sonny was always talking about me, always saying how much he loved me. I wished that he would say it
to me as much as he was telling the world, but it still made me
happy to know.*

*I remember how, when we first got married, your daddy would
come home and we would sit up playing cards in bed or watching our little t.v. We had some good times. And you kids were
his heart. You still are. Think about all those things we do together as a family, how we take you all to ride the ponies or to
the amusement park; how your daddy picks you up from school
and buys you all a treat every day. Think about the good times,
honey, and forgive your daddy. So many people pull him in all
these different directions. I want something from him, his mama
wants something, his friends expect him to be a certain way for
them, and sometimes your daddy loses himself trying to be all
the things people want him to be.*

*But I remember him, how it used to be, and I stand here crying
and screaming after him to try to get him to remember. That's
why I don't leave. I want him to turn around and remember me,
and his kids; to come back and get all this love that I've been sav-
ing for him . . .*

And one day Daddy did turn around and walk back into
Mom's arms. But not before Mom got tired of waiting for him
to remember her, and her voice had run dry, her tears fossil-
ized into skeletons of yearning. Not before she packed her life
and her children into the back of her old broken-down Simca,

the car she had bought for herself before she got married, and drove across town to our new house, which she also bought and fixed up on her own. And not before his heart had swelled to the size of his rib cage and he started having visions of a mountain that he couldn't climb over.

Only then, in the weeks before he died, could Daddy see himself clearly and the good thing he had in Mom. They curled up in his hospital bed, watched the tiny t.v. on the wall of his room, and slept facing one another at night, breathing each other's breath. They forgave one another between spoonfuls of Jello and glasses of juice and water held tenderly to feeble lips. Mom says that after Daddy died, she didn't hold onto the anger. She simply loved him and accepted the love he was finally able to give.

When I visited him in the hospital, I saw the way he looked at me, as if I was the most perfect thing in his life. We teased one another like old friends, and when he hugged me, I felt again like a baby, safe, sheltered in his largeness. And then he was gone. The night he died, I felt a chill run over my body, and I knew it was him visiting me for the last time. I died too, that night, our souls crossed above my body, and whatever I remembered of him then, I willed myself to forget, willed my heart into silence. He was lost to me, like the balloons that always escaped from my wrists at the zoo. I wanted it to be that simple, to be able to cut away, let go of, those parts of my life that seemed too painful.

And even now, I find myself searching the eyes of strangers for a man whose gaze offers the possibility of the way Daddy looked at me before he died; trying to curl up in arms that can't hold me, combing the sky for stray spots of color.

For you
loudman daddyman thief
lover of bottles like wives

I swallow nights
of your alcoholic breath
dislodging me from sleep;
of mama's hip,
bruised when the cigarettes
were all gone

We forgave
those nights like scars
against our tongues

We forgave
broken kitchen glass,
the wet spot in your pants
as if age had lost you,
had sent you back
to where you couldn't quite remember
how letters came together,
and numbers were only fingers

We forgave
until forgiving was just wanting
and wanting was only waiting
for morning to come

To you
loser of houses,
of babies misborn

this is just to say
we are alive
daddy


and the days keep coming
in the space where you took to the earth
your bloated heart,
where you left me
in the midst of twelve years


To you
lifegiver
i loved you like fire


but i like you best
when you are sleeping


# VIII

I have always had high hopes for love. I come from a family
where falling in love is as natural as walking, inevitable as the
sun rising and setting on every day.

When I was very young, before my father died, before the
men in our family began to disappear, the walls of our house
reverberated with their presence. I remember family gatherings at my grandmother Nana's house when all the chairs
were full, and people overflowed into almost every room and
empty place in the house, balancing plates on their knees or
in their hands, after we had sweated prayers into one another's palms, heads bowed; new dress, old suit itching;
mouths full of hunger we had saved all day.

Once the gumbo chicken bones, and the crab and crawfish
shells had been collected and wrapped in old newspapers

from the back porch, and all that was left on our plates was a thin river of blood-colored juice from the cranberry sauce, running red over scraps of dressing and turkey, discarded elbows of macaroni and stray black-eyed peas, we pushed back from the table and went our separate ways.

Sometimes I was part of the long train of women headed back to the kitchen, arms full of half-eaten food and empty plates, their voices looping around my waist, dragging me into the leftover heat. The men headed in the opposite direction, tumbling toward the living room, where they pushed Nana's coffee tables up against the walls to accommodate their legs. Long legs stretched out from armchairs and the sofa, almost meeting in the center of the small room, the bodies attached to them like points on some awkward star, or spokes on a wheel turning slowly as they rotated chairs or shifted positions. Some of the other men would descend to the basement, where they opened card tables and beers and shouted up through the floor lest we forget them. *Hey, somebody turn the music up! Tell one of the kids to bring me another beer . . . and a slice of pie! Hey, can you all hear us down here?!*

Love was in my blood, love was out there waiting for me. It was only a matter of opening my door, so that love could come in. I knew this was so, because it had happened before, when my grandfather came knocking on my grandmother's door selling portraits; he fell in love just seeing her out of the corner of his eye as he tried to persuade her father to buy one of his pictures. It happened for my great-aunt Rowena, Nana's sister, when her husband-to-be, a jazz musician, left love letters and songs at her doorstep every morning. It had even happened for my mother, when she walked into her living room and met my father who was there playing cards with her brother.

I expected to hear love's heavy footsteps coming up the walkway, his firm knock. I covered myself in my best oils and left the door open a crack, so that the fragrance of my sweet-smelling self could escape and entice him to come in. I left poems hanging on the front gate.

By the time I was ready to look for love, the path was already worn and marred, full of pockmarks from the countless stops and starts, the movement and brief periods of rest of a changing society and black community. My sisters and brother and I, born during the seventies, entered a society in the process of reinventing itself. Although there had been movement and transition before, it was movement of a different kind. During the migration of black Southerners to the North, the movement seemed to be toward one another, as the newly arrived sought out color as soon as the train or car or bus lurched to a halt; held their breath until they reached the familiar smells and sounds of food and music pouring out of open windows and doorways; the neighborhoods, like webs woven into an intricate pattern of dreams and desires held in common.

But as these dreams began to poke beyond the neighborhoods, in the rumblings before and in the largeness of space to be filled after the Civil Rights and Women's movements, as the heavy print of the "I" of integration began to stamp out the "we," the direction of the wind began to change. People were blowing out of the neighborhoods instead of in. We were born in this wind, part of the long trail of black folks climbing the ladder towards middle class, towards better, towards more.

But I thought I knew what to look for and how to find it. I believed in the love spells, the sacred songs, the stories that had been handed down to me; believed that they would lead me to the kind of love I saw in movies, where the man's eyes glaze over as he stares at the woman he's chosen, as though she's the only other person on the planet, or something holy. The kind of love promised in Mom's arms, when my heart deflated and sagged, a paper bag somebody blew up then punched all the air out of. *He wasn't right for you. You deserve better. The right man will come along, and, when he does, things will be different. He won't hurt you, he'll make you happy.*

The love I prayed for in the darkness of my room, surrendering to the winding curves and long notes of Nina Simone and Donny Hathaway, imagining another dark body encircling me, enclosing me in his warmth, in the comfortable place our bodies would make.

## IX

A history of motion swirled at my feet, as I looked for something to steady myself. I reached for him at the beginning of my freshman year of high school. Him, the awkward-looking white boy in my homeroom who sat on the opposite side of the room, three tables over. He was a kind of grungy median between punk rock and heavy metal. He wore his hair in some version of a mohawk, long on top, shaved on either side, with a tail stretching all the way to the small of his back. He dressed the same almost every day, in a faded T-shirt bearing the name of some heavy metal or hard-core band, black Levi's, red high-top Converse All-Stars and a long army-green trench coat.

All of this appealed to me, for I had entered my own "punk-rock phase" during eighth grade, when my friend and I started going to Smiths, Cure and Depeche Mode concerts draped in black: black clothes, black nail polish, and black eyeliner, which extended beyond our eyes in heavy lines drawn up to our temples, or down the sides of our faces in spider-web designs.

Whenever I glanced over at him, he was engrossed in his book or his homework, in a place all by himself. He looked like I felt. I called out to him with my eyes. He didn't respond, so I went back to my family's mojo, back to what I had learned from the women about getting a man's attention. I wore all my best "punk rock" outfits—combat boots with a Ralph Lauren skirt, army fatigues and jeans ripped at the knees with my favorite Jones New York jacket. My hair was saturated with mousse and gel so that it would hold the style I achieved in the morning by bending over and shaking my head until my hair scattered in all directions. I paraded past his table, taking the long way over to my seat.

Still no response. But my eyes kept veering over to his side of the room; kept seeking him out day after day. I called him the "mohawk guy" in my journal. My fascination with him was a luxury. I began to watch him closely, noting the way his lips poked out slightly as he read, or the way the breeze from the open window sometimes lifted the hair on top of his head, and how he would use both hands to flatten it. I studied his movements, started to know him through these small things, and then I learned his name.

One afternoon, we were standing near one another as we crowded around the doorway with the rest of our homeroom class, waiting for the last bell to ring. I noticed that he had written his address and phone number on the i.d. tag dangling from his backpack. I copied down both. When I got home that same afternoon, my sister called him claiming to be the Messiah. And so began an elaborate series of phone calls in which we, in addition to impersonating Jesus Christ, faked British accents, sent him to the school library during one of his study periods to meet a girl who didn't exist, and created another who only existed on the phone, but to whom he sent notes. Guess who was the messenger? The calls and the note-writing got his attention, and I, after much explaining and sorting out of details, got him.

We went to the movies and hung out at shopping malls. On Fridays, I joined his family in their weekly ritual of going out for Chinese, and he became a fixture at my house. We had intense make-out sessions in each other's bedrooms when our parents weren't at home—and sometimes when they were. We made up stupid pet names for each other and fantasized about getting married and having children. He was the first man I made love with.

"Why doesn't he bring you home when you go out?" Mom would erupt as soon as I walked into the house after an evening out with him. No matter what, I always found myself rushing to explain on his behalf.

"Well, when we're with his parents they always drop me off."

"I'm talking about when it's just the two of you, like tonight."

"I told you Mom, he doesn't have his own car and he can't drive his parents', so we have to take the train. But he rides with me back to my stop."

"Well, he should walk you to your door, then. Whenever he comes over here, you walk him up to the train station."

"It's only a couple of blocks."

"But then you have to walk back by yourself. And when he drops you off at your stop, you still have to walk home by yourself. It's dark outside, and if it was broad daylight, that doesn't make it right." I am remembering leaning on his shoulder in the dark of the theater, the warmth of his mouth everywhere . . .

"It's not that late. There are still people out."

"You know that's not my point."

"Well, he doesn't have money. If he got off to walk me, he'd have to pay again."

"And you have money?"

"No, but I don't have to pay again."

"You mean to tell me, he's got money to go out, but he can't get on the train? Does he at least treat you when you're out?"

"Sometimes."

"Why not all the time?"

"I told you, he doesn't have any money." I'm remembering the time we went to visit his mom's office, and she gave him a twenty dollar bill to take me out to lunch. We decided to stop at a fast-food place. His lunch came to five dollars, mine came to three. He paid for his and kept the rest. There was a comic book he wanted to buy that cost thirteen dollars, plus tax . . .

"When I was growing up, and to this day, if a man takes me out, I don't even look at my purse."

"Well, it's not like that anymore."

"It's certainly not going to be that way if you don't start it off like that. You girls are out here chasing after these boys, and what does it get you?"

I am remembering the rose lying across his pillow for me the first time we made love. I am remembering the way his voice goes soft when he says my name . . .

"I'm telling you, you can talk that liberated woman stuff all you want, but I think it's bullshit. Men still expect to do those things. But even the good ones, if they see you don't expect them to take you home or pay for your dinner, they're not going to do it. You have to set the stage for that."

"But I don't want to spend my life depending on some man. I can take care of myself."

"Look, I'm not saying you can't be independent. But when

you're with someone who claims to care about you, you should feel like the most important person in the world. You should feel that anyway, but especially then. This is not about the money, it's about him treating you with the respect and consideration that you deserve."

I remember that feeling of embarrassment, in line at the movies or at dinner, watching the men in other couples reach for their wallets, while I ordered my own ticket at the window or calculated my portion of the check. It wasn't that I minded spending the money, but I remember, too, wondering, does he think I'm special? If he thought I was special would he pay for dinner? And although I tried to keep focused on the good things he did, all of those things together could not wipe away that wondering, the questions that kept spinning, unvoiced, at the back of my throat.

## X

*1957. My mother, as the girl she was before she became my mother, leans against the wall in a church basement decorated with streamers and balloons. The room is crowded with teenagers dancing close, chaperones pulling them apart. She has been dancing all night, and now she is resting. One boy after another walks up to her and holds out his hand. Queen of the Pastor's Tea, queen of the prom, everybody wants to dance with her. But she fans them away. Can't they see she's tired?*

*Along this wall are also standing the girls who weren't asked and who wouldn't ask a young man for a dance. Could she be one of them, my mother leaning against the wall? Maybe she has only danced in the stories she will tell of this night, in the reflection she sees, staring wistfully at the floor, keeping time to the music with a soft tap of her newly polished saddle shoes.*

Play another slow jam, this time make it sweet . . .

Sixth grade, seventh grade, eighth grade school dances, my song was always playing. As ice cream in styrofoam bowls melted into muddy rivers, I stood along the sidelines, at the edge of sound, searching for a loose seam in the music that I could pull apart and enter.

I waited for love to come strutting up in new shoes, burning under the smell of his daddy's cologne. I waited for your hand, cool clay against my face. I have been in rooms swollen twice their size with possibility and I have looked for you in the largeness. Rooms shaking with wordless music. That's where I was told I'd find you. You emerging out of a smoke screen of desire, a wilderness of restless years, and I was promised that you'd be looking for me. But beneath the music I was still, encased in a capsule of longing; the story of my life, a hieroglyph of flattened bone and crystallized pop songs, imprinted along the wall.

There were hours, years even, that led up to this waiting. There were days of choosing the perfect outfit to wear. There were nights of planning what he would whisper in my ear as his fingers clung to my hips and the music swirled at our awkward feet. Do you understand? I had to train to hope like this; to walk the room shrouded in indifference; to pass the shadows of intertwined couples, the fantasy that left me behind, and not blink. And the days and the nights last and last; the school dances become proms and formals and night-clubs, but the songs keep turning over in my jukebox of a heart.

There were times when you came to me briefly; there were moments of your smiles; there was heat when we pressed together. Your hands were cupped with water. I kept these moments. You live in these moments. I saved you, when I was a scream thrown against a glass wall of music, a flower pressed against brick and mortar, still pretty, even after all the water was gone, just before petals crumbled to ash. My family's love stories looming large above my head, a portrait, a disappointed moon.

## XI

I met him in a bookstore, on an ordinary day, a day that I least expected someone to be smiling at me when I looked up from the book I had been flipping through. But there he was. He would not have been my first choice, as far as looks. I liked skinny, artsy black boys, the ones wearing faded jeans and dreadlocks, who emitted frankincense like sweat. He definitely didn't look artsy, but I liked the way his closely cropped hair showed off the nice even roundness of his head; the way his jeans sagged b-boy style in opposition to the crisp white shirt and tie he was wearing. Two broad silver bracelets jangled on his wrists. His skin made me think of bread, the color of pumpernickel or dark rye. And he was smiling at me. This is what appealed to me most of all. I smiled back.

He offered to buy me a cup of coffee at the small cafe in the corner of the store. I refused the drink but was impressed enough to sit down and talk. He seemed different. He was from Africa. I could hear in his accent his connection to someplace else, like the South my family had migrated from. The South which moved in their voices like water beneath a layer of thin ice. Except his was a South that spilled over into his laughter and drenched me in its warmth. I loved the twists and turns of his accent, the way his voice rose and fell when he said my name. He complimented me on my African head wrap and my nose ring. He had been in the city three years working at a nearby coffeeshop to put himself through college, where he was studying computer technology.

I asked him if he was interested in the arts. He shrugged

and said that he loved listening to music but had not had very much exposure to anything else. My smile fell a little when I heard that, but then I remembered something my mother was always telling me, "You spend all this time pining over these artists, only to find out that they aren't the kind of people who are good for you." (This was true.) "All the while, you could be missing some guy in a suit or some computer nerd trying to get your attention, who may not be a writer or a musician, but who adores you."

Maybe I shouldn't write this guy off so quickly, I thought. He seemed nice enough, respectful. Maybe our differences would make things more interesting. We exchanged numbers. The courtship rituals of my "twenty-something" generation were crass, by and large, nothing left to the imagination, no subtlety of approach. But there was something about him that reminded me of the old days I had never lived through, only heard about and yearned for. Maybe it was the way he shyly lowered his eyes when he spoke to me, his tone hovering just above a whisper; or the way he listened to me with his head cocked and his hands folded in front of him.

A month into the relationship, he was spending the night at my dorm room regularly. When school let out for the summer, he helped me move into my new apartment and moved himself in as well, although he kept his old place. I could feel myself changing, my body folding around his like clay, my smile, my laugh, becoming seamless. Just as liquid takes on the shape of its container, I transformed to fit the shape of his needs and desires.

I squeezed my clothes into drawers and boxes so that he could have closet space. I moved my computer to the floor and let him put his on my desk. I planned my day around his schedule. If I went to the library, I finished my work by the time he got off so that we could ride the train home together.

If I didn't go out during the day, I had dinner ready when he came home.

When had finding love become as urgent as breathing? When had it become the metronome dictating the rhythm of my heartbeat? I had listened to my mother and my grand-mothers telling me to give but also to keep something for my-self, to hold on and to know when to let go. I didn't know how to do what they were trying to teach me. I didn't see it in their lives. I had watched some of the women in my family sink into the emptiness that lost love had left behind, and I had watched others build their lives alone. I had seen them fight and beg to be loved and I had watched them surrender. I couldn't find the balance.

## XII

I looked around the terminal at black folks from every corner of the United States, many already draped in colorful over-sized African attire, as we waited to board our flight to Ghana. I listened to snatches of conversations around me, the stories people told of their coming to this place. Somehow I thought this day would be more important than any other day, would be the day that the memories of the past that lived deep within me, buried beneath forgetful years, would come alive again.

We followed the sound of the drum. And the drum led us to the edge of the world as we knew it. Here we stood, look-ing across the ocean to a world we hoped to discover. Africa. I thought of how much we had invested in this place, how desperately we wanted it to be the thing that soothed the ache of not knowing our beginnings, the ache that we carried like restless spirits seeking resolution, a resting place. Africa was the wish, our greatest hope for salvation, for certainty that we belonged somewhere. We had constructed our own Africa as we needed it to be. We braid our hair and wear the flowing garments. Africa, help us to see you more clearly, so that we may also see ourselves.

We closed our eyes, as one foot after the other left solid ground. We spiraled into blackness, traveling backwards to the unknown, to memory, *Africa, will it be your arms that catch our fall?*

As we made our descent into Accra, the concrete and pollution-gray morning of our departure the day before had become the bronze-tinted mist of this morning's sunrise over the flat Ghanaian landscape; the crossing of an ocean reduced to the blink of an eye. When we touched down, a faint wave of applause rose up and died before it got to our cabin. More than remembrance, Mom and I felt relief at having reached the ground safely, the anticipation of sleep more than the excitement of discovery.

Outside of the plane there were no welcome signs, no drums beating the news of our arrival, only the disgruntled and sleepy ground crew speaking to one another in harsh sounding whispers, as they ushered us into a shuttle bus waiting to drive us the few steps over to the main terminal where we would collect our luggage and meet our tour guides. I looked around for something to grab hold of that would ground me in this place, some small sign of recognition. I looked into the faces of the people I passed as I walked down the steps from the plane, and as I boarded the bus, but their eyes would not meet mine.

At the baggage terminal, we were met by our Ghanaian tour guides, two tall and slender young men in their mid-twenties, who stood like guard posts alongside us. One smiled all the time, the other barely said a word. I looked to them, grateful for their presence and hopeful that they would provide the anchor, the link to this place for which I was searching. But both seemed equally far away, untouchable. The silent one stared off into the distance, over our heads, perhaps looking to the hour when he would be relieved of his tedious duty.

The smiling one chatted while we waited for our luggage. He welcomed us to Accra, asked the usual questions: how was our flight, what was the weather like in the States, was this our first time in Africa. He had us figured: black tourists, searching for our people, our origins; searching for more than he chose or was able to give. He was not there to offer sympathy or to hold our hands along this preposterous journey, or to point us in the right direction. He was there simply to make sure we got to the hotel on time, to develop an itinerary and to see that we stuck to it with as few glitches as possible.

I couldn't deny the distance I felt from this ambitious young man, a distance in which the lines separating businessman and client were clear and indisputable, as was the barrier he had erected around himself to keep us out. And in this way, we were also held captive in his notions of "us," of what we wanted and why we came. He had seen enough of "us" to know that we too would cage him if he wasn't careful, that we would penetrate the surface of his skin with our keen yearnings, with the unyielding eye of the scientist, until we reached the chapel of bone; that we could unclench his pounding fist of a heart, until the blood flowed freely; that, given the chance, we would drink him dry.

Our bags finally rolled around on the squeaky conveyer belt. The tour guides stacked them one by one onto the cart they had brought along. At the customs checkpoint before the exit, they waved a rumpled piece of paper in front of the officials and we breezed through with only a flash of our passports. Before we left the terminal, our guide warned us to watch our bags and not to give anyone any money. So began my heart's slow descent. I had not come all this way to watch my bag. I had come to feel at home, hoping for an alternative to the home I had left where you always had to be careful, where there was no place safe.

Outside, a throng of people waited. They seemed to spring to life as soon as we appeared. What felt like a million eyes turned to us. We stood at the crowd's edge, suspended in a moment of curiosity and panic, before we too were jolted into action, pulled into its midst. We swam through the bodies in staccato motion, each step a collage of disjointed movements, looking the way my sisters and brother and I used to look dancing in the dark of our basement, one of us waving a flashlight rapidly, watching the flickering light turn our bodies into robots. "Can you feel it?" we always asked the one taking his or her turn in front of the light, for the light made our bodies look so cumbersome, made even the slightest finger snap look as though it required all of our energy and the coordination of our entire body to achieve.

But this time I really could feel it. My body was a weight that I dragged through the blurred motion of the crowd closing in around me. *Hunger.* Our two tour guides made their narrow bodies into walls to shield us as they ushered us through the mob. *Goes both ways.* I don't remember faces, just hands reaching, teeth bared, and wondering what I had that they wanted. Mom's fingers gripped my wrist tightly, planting there the red imprint of her terror. One woman rushed up to us with a bunch of wilted flowers she wanted to pin on our collars in exchange for a small contribution. Another man, begging for change, began to help our guides unload our luggage into the silver VW minivan waiting to take us to the hotel.

Inside the van, we were sealed off from the throbbing crowd outside. The sliding door clicked shut and the only sounds were the soft whir of the motor, the wind of the air conditioning blowing into our faces. Part of me wanted to open the door and fling myself into those arms, just to feel them touching me, me touching them, to inhale the scent of the people, let the dust, which left everything covered in its copper-colored kisses, cake on my skin. Instead I sank deeper into the van's comfortable seats, thankful for the quiet and the cool breeze drying the sweat on my forehead.

Our tour guides had assumed their positions. The quiet one took the wheel. The other, sitting next to him, who introduced himself as Kwame, turned to face us. His wide smile beckoned us like a magnet, drawing our eyes away from the man outside who had begun pounding on our windows begging for money; distracting us from the reawakening realization that we were far from home, and that if we called out there was nobody to claim the sound of our voices. The smile, which was at once friendly and capable of eating us alive, was all we had to rely on. "Akwaaba," Kwame said. "This means welcome. Welcome to Africa."

We stumbled into our hotel thinking only of sleep. As Kwame checked us in, we sank exhausted into the lobby's plush couches and armchairs. Upstairs in our room, Mom and I could finally relax, shedding our luggage and layers of winter clothes. I went to the window and pulled back the heavy curtains, still trying to convince myself that I was really here. Someone could have made it all up, like some huge movie set with thousands of extras hired to fill up the streets and meet us at the airport; a tourist trap, to cash in on our hunger. I let the curtain fall back into place, blocking out the light from outside. Just as Accra was coming awake, I fell into bed, hoping that it would all still be there waiting for me when I got up.

Shortly after four o'clock, Mom and I were awakened by the telephone. It was Mary, a Ghanaian tour guide whom we had not yet met. She wanted to know if we would be interested in taking a trip to a seamstress or to a hair braider. I had planned to get my hair rebraided and have some traditional African clothing made while I was here, but Mom wasn't ready to get up yet. She had already fallen back asleep, having only opened her eyes long enough to find out who was on the phone and to comment, "They sure don't waste any time trying to get you to spend your money." Disappointed, I told Mary that we would wait until another time.

By the time we got up, dressed, and made our way downstairs to meet the rest of our group for dinner, the lobby had been transformed for a cocktail party. There were several tables set up with cool drinks, manned by the waiters I had seen from my window this morning darting around the pool. Mom nudged me towards one of the tables. Neither of us had had anything to eat or drink since breakfast on the plane. I stood before the table surveying my choices and ordered two glasses of fruit punch. The waiter smiled flirtatiously as he ladled the pink liquid into tall frosted glasses.

"For you and your boyfriend?" he asked slyly.

"For me and my mom," I answered, flirting back.

"Where is your boyfriend?"

"At home."

"Where is home?"

"Washington, DC."

"What about Africa? You don't consider Africa home?" he admonished, handing me the drinks. Our fingers touched as I took them. "Let me tell you, " he said, lowering his voice into that sexy register, just above a whisper. "You are home now. And for a new home, you need a new man, mmm?"

"I don't think my boyfriend would appreciate that," I said, turning to walk away. "But thanks for the drinks." He nodded and shifted his attention to the next person in line. I rolled my eyes at the cheap pick-up lines he probably tried on every woman who came to his table.

"What are you grinning about?" my mother asked when I got back to the spot she had staked out by the automatic doors leading out to the courtyard. I shrugged my shoulders. I hadn't realized I was grinning.

On the morning of our third day, I woke before sunrise to the bright orange tip of Mom's lighted cigarette, flickering in one spot and then another as she paced around the room.

"What's wrong, Ma?" I asked, sitting up in bed.

"I had this dream," Mom said, turning on the light, "that we were going to be kidnapped." I laughed out loud at how ridiculous this sounded. Mom joined me in my laughter. And for a moment, it was like it always was when we had bad dreams, how once we were awake and could laugh about them, everything was alright, the terror we had felt explained away.

"No, I'm serious," Mom said sitting close to me on the bed, her smile fading. "It was so real. These men were trying to take us away and nobody knew where we were. They wouldn't let us go home."

"Why would anyone want to kidnap us?" I asked, annoyed. Mom always blew everything out of proportion, worried intensely with even the slightest provocation. I didn't want to go through this now, not here. This morning we were leaving Accra for Cape Coast, the site of one of the major holding castles where captured Africans were kept in dungeons before being shipped across the Atlantic Ocean and delivered into slavery. I was especially looking forward to seeing the castles and possibly doing some research on the slave trade from the African perspective.

"Why would anyone want to kidnap us?" I asked again.

"I don't know," Mom sighed. "In my dream, they really only wanted you."

On the way to Cape Coast, we pulled over onto the gravel shoulder of the highway at the outskirts of a small fishing village, a smattering of thatched-roof huts made of mud, leaves, and straw. This was to be an unscheduled stop, our tour guide announced, even though it had been clearly printed on the itinerary that we received at the beginning of the tour: *Stop At Local Village En Route To Cape Coast.*

"In our culture, it is customary to bring a gift to the chief whenever one visits his village," our guide explained. "Normally, we would present the chief with a gift of Schnapps," she continued, "but since we are arriving unexpectedly, we should give a small monetary offering."

"What kind of culture is that?"someone from our group snorted.

"We call it hustling in the States," someone cracked, and a ripple of laughter spread through the group. Reluctantly, we reached into our pockets and produced a few thousand cedis each (one thousand cedis was roughly equivalent to one American dollar). The tour guide ignored the jokes and the sarcasm as she collected the sweaty, crumpled bills. She counted the money, then walked up to the edge of the village where a lanky teenage boy, dressed in a long-sleeved Western-style button-down shirt and shorts, emerged to meet her. The boy, we were told when our guide rejoined our group, was the nephew of the chief and would present our offering to his uncle. We would know when he returned whether or not the chief had granted us permission to enter the village.

While we waited, I took a few pictures. From where we stood, the village looked like a ghost town. The chief's nephew was the only person we had seen moving throughout the sparse cluster of huts. He reappeared momentarily and began walking toward our group, waving us into the village.

As we entered, we were met by a few of the tribesmen and a small brigade of children, all dressed in dingy Western clothing. Most of the men wore cotton button-down shirts and shorts, like the chief's nephew. The women we passed, most dressed in silk-screened T-shirts and wrap skirts made from African cloth, lingered in the doorways of the huts, or watched from where they sat washing or cooking in their front yards. A girl of about eight and a boy around five or six sidled up to me. The girl, dressed in a faded yellow Sunday dress, casually slipped her hand into mine and asked me where I was from.

"The United States," I answered.

"Oh," she nodded, "I like that place."

"Have you been there?" I asked.

"No, but I've heard of it." She reached into her dress pocket and produced a small square of white paper on which her name and address had been written, I assumed, by a more adult hand than hers. "Will you write me?" she asked. I told her I would and tucked the paper into my notebook.

"Maybe you will bring me there for a visit sometime," she

said, letting go of my hand and skipping up to the woman walking ahead of me. I saw her give this woman a square of paper just like the one she had given me.

The little boy stayed behind, his eyes on the camera dangling around my neck.

"What do you call it?" he asked, pointing.

"A camera," I answered.

"May I hold it?" I took the camera off of its strap and placed it cautiously in his tiny hands. He turned it over a few times, looking first through the wide lens in the front, and then the small window of the viewfinder. "May I keep it?" he beamed up at me.

"I'm sorry, this is the only camera I have," I said, taking the camera.

"Then maybe you can send me one." He produced a square of paper similar to the girl's and handed it to me. His name, too, had been written by an adult hand.

We were led to the chief's meeting house, a one-room cottage, cool and dark, bare except for two wooden benches running the length of each wall and a smaller bench positioned at the front of the room. The children, who had not entered the house with us, peered at us through the windows, their scrawny arms dangling into the room through the uncovered, paneless openings roughly cut out of the mud walls.

After we were settled on the benches along the wall, the chief and his linguist entered the house. The linguist was the only one who could speak directly to the chief. Our guide introduced us to the linguist, who then addressed the chief. The chief spoke and the linguist translated his greeting. We were told that other groups of black Americans and black British tourists had visited the village. So much for an unscheduled stop.

"The chief would like you to know how happy he is that

you have all come home," the linguist said. The chief spoke again, extending his arms and gesturing wildly. Again, the linguist interpreted for us.

"Many years ago, strangers came to our land and took our people. Some of us sold our own people to these strange men. But we didn't know what would happen to those who were sold away. We didn't know. And by the time we had learned the horrors of what our people were experiencing over there, across the water, it was too late. We are so sorry we let you go. But we never gave up hoping that you would come back, that we would see you again. Welcome home, my lost sisters and brothers, Akwaaba."

The linguist then walked around the room and gave each of us a Ghanaian name, speculating on the tribe from which we were descended. When he got to me, he held my hand in his. I could smell the alcohol on his breath. He had been staring at me the entire time we were there. He gave me the name Aku, which means, "born on a Wednesday," and then said, "Aku is not going back home. She will stay here with me." I stiffened, not wanting to look at Mom.

Mom grabbed my hand from his. "You can't have her," she said hysterically. "This is my daughter!" The rest of the group laughed nervously. The linguist silently locked eyes with Mom.

"Why don't we go outside?"our tour guide suggested, breaking the tension. "The chief will be available for photographs." We lined up to take a picture with the chief. Afterwards, we went on a tour of the village. Mom walked close beside me, the linguist on my other side.

"Hold my hand and walk with me," he said, taking my hand. Mom grabbed me by my free arm. One of the men from our group, seeing how upset Mom was, walked up to the linguist and put his hand on his shoulder to lead him away.

"Come on man, leave her alone. This is a married woman," he lied. The linguist again fixed his red-eyed gaze on Mom before walking ahead to lead the tour.

After leaving the village, we dropped our luggage off at the rooming house where we would be sleeping that night. The hotel where we were supposed to stay had double-booked our rooms and didn't have any others available. We ate a dinner of greasy "Ghanaian style" fried chicken and then came to the evening's event, a march to commemorate slavery.

The minivan dropped us off at the foot of a steep hill. Cape Coast loomed above us. With Mary and Kwame leading the way, we began the climb, winding through the narrow streets. The stench from the open sewage lines dug on either side of the road was unbearable, and it was so dark I could only make out the rough silhouettes of houses and people.

We reached the top of the hill and walked into a wide clearing where a crowd had gathered. Some people were holding torches, others flashlights and candles. A voice speaking in French sounded over a loudspeaker. "They're telling the story of slavery," I heard a nearby tour guide translating for his group. Suddenly the mass of bodies started moving. I allowed myself to be pushed along with it.

There was music now, streaming over our heads. The locals in the crowd began to dance. A dance that was more like running, feet sliding along the pavement. Three steps forward, one back. On the one step back, the entire body would lean backwards, suspended, as though surrendering to a strong wind, then snap upright, curving slightly, head down, fighting this same wind to move forward. Three steps forward, one back. Us, I thought. This is us. History. The body remembers. Though the people dancing seemed to be doing so only for the pleasure of it, perhaps performing for the foreigners in their midst, not grasping or searching for any meaning.

I faced the night and the flickering throng shining against it. I wanted to join them. I wanted to dance. But I could feel Mom behind me, struggling to stay close as she clung to the straps of my backpack. She was still shaken from earlier, the village, the dream, and had stayed close to me all day. She was suffocating me, and I was angry at her for not being able to control her fear.

"Can't you see how ridiculous this is?" I lashed out at her.

"I know, I know, but I can't get rid of this feeling." Over dinner, she had shared her dream with the rest of our group. "You see how nobody questioned the possibility. Nobody ever said that it wouldn't happen," she reminded me.

"I guess they're all in on the plan to kidnap me," I said sarcastically.

"What are you looking for here? What do you want from this place?" Mom asked me later, once we were alone in our room.

"I don't know," I said. "I'm just sick of always feeling like I'm floating. I want to be settled, happy . . ."

"You think you're going to find that here?"

"I didn't say I was going to find anything here, I just wanted to see what this place has to offer," I said, exasperated.

"The people here don't even know what they have to offer!" Mom railed. "Look at that village. The men were all drunk, the kids were begging. And that crock of bull they fed us about slavery. These people don't care anything about slavery."

The night before we left Accra, our group had attended a

lecture given by a Ghanaian scholar on the history of various tribes in Ghana. When I asked how the slave trade had impacted the people of Ghana, the man was evasive. In his tribe, slavery was not something that was discussed, nor was it taught to children in school. Their history courses still focused primarily on Europe, one of the lasting effects of colonization. "We have a saying," he told us. " 'All that you need to know is right in front of you.' There is no need to look back."

# XIII

He was already asleep, beads of sweat rolling off the smooth, muscular curves of his back. The loneliness which seeped into my bones and weighed down my head made my shoulders slouch as I climbed out of the bed where I had been lying beside him. I wanted to run, knowing that there was nowhere else for me to go. I was alone in the city. Two years ago, I had drifted to DC to go to law school, discomfited by the lack of security writing offered. I hadn't felt rooted or made a home of this place. I had mostly filled my days and my nights with him.

I felt anger rising up from the loneliness, as I studied the outline of his body curled into a fetal position, his back, a closed door, turned to me as it so often was after the few moments he held me when our lovemaking was finished, when our bodies split into two separate entities carving out and negotiating our own space on my queen-sized bed. Anger at the fact that he was the one I turned to when I needed someone. He was the one I looked forward to seeing at the end of the day and waking up next to in the morning. Now when I needed him to reach for me in the darkness, pull me close, he was fast asleep.

When we first moved in together, I relished these moments when everything in the apartment settled down and it was just me wandering through silence. That was my best thinking and writing time. But lately, I missed the company, the distraction of somebody else's voice or thoughts breaking into mine. I get so anxious when I'm alone.

It was this book that I was working on. Those little pokes and pinches of doubt, the usual anxieties most writers experience before starting a new project, had spiraled out of control. The book, or, more accurately, the fear that I wouldn't be able to write it, had become this monumental thing that I couldn't seem to break down into manageable pieces. I felt so empty, as though I'd lost my voice, the sound that once resonated so clearly in my head, that let me know the parts of my brain and my heart where the ideas and the poems were born were still alive and working. Words no longer kept me company.

The phone rang around three that morning. I was just starting to feel tired when that awful sound ripped through the dark and grabbed me around the neck, stopping my breath for the split second it took me to reach over and pick up the receiver. My heart started racing. It wasn't every time the phone rang late at night that I had such an extreme reaction. Usually it was Mom or a friend calling. But I had learned from the call that came when my father died, there are certain sounds that signal disaster, a certain way the phone can ring that echoes like a scream.

It was Mom on the other end, calling from Boston. She started talking as soon as she heard my voice, before I could even ask her what was going on. "The doctors called this morning / breath / Nana's not doing too well / breath / I'm on my way to the airport / breath / If you want to come you should / breath / come now. Call the airlines and make sure you tell them you have a family emergency / breath / Call the hospital and tell them to let Nana know that you're coming / breath / I'll call you when I get there."

She was on her way to the airport, three hours before her flight was scheduled to depart. She didn't want to be near the phone or know anything else before she got to Chicago. I could hear her shedding her thick mother skin, peeling back to the fragile layers of daughter.

I hung up the phone gently, deliberately, allowing time for the news Mom had just given me to settle into my consciousness. Word by breathless word, the pieces came together, shrieking across the screen of my eyelids. My grandmother, Nana, who had been in the hospital for three months now, was struggling for her life. It was my worst fear, the hollow of guilt carved in the small of my back, given substance, shape, a name; the fear that had grown in me since I left home to move into my own apartment in DC, that something would go wrong, something would happen to someone in my family, and I wouldn't be there. And then, too, there was this new dread, overtaking the old, that maybe I would.

I picked up the phone again and made my flight reservations. I wouldn't be leaving until the afternoon. My body sprang into motion. I went to the kitchen, turned on the water, turned off the water. Went into the bathroom, flipped the light off then on again. Headed back to the bedroom. He was still asleep. I couldn't stand to hear the steadiness of his breathing. It was such a sharp contradiction to my mood. Felt like a slap in the face. I didn't wake him.

My pacing ended abruptly in front of the stereo and I began to sift through the tapes and CDs scattered at my feet. I searched for the old songs, monuments of the past that I could lean on. I stretched out flat on the floor, pressing my back into the thin layer of carpet which provided only a slight cushion between me and the hard wood beneath it. Fingertips of music poked and kneaded and caressed until my body lost all boundaries and everything in me was soft.

I like to think we eased one another's passage, my cousin who met me at the airport, and I, who came. I like to think we kept each other company in those moments of suspension, of transition from one part of our lives to the next. He saw me first, picked me out of the throng of lights and faces which to me was just a blur of color and sound.

We hugged and he took my bag. Walking through the terminal, we kept brushing up against each other. I remembered the way we used to be together. We were born twenty days apart; I'm the oldest. He used to tell everyone that I was his sister, but that was a long time ago. We barely kept in touch now. How many years had it been since we had even talked? Neither of us knew. Neither of us had bothered counting.

I couldn't stop thinking about something Toni Morrison said about how the flooding of rivers is not flooding at all, it's remembering. "Remembering where it used to be." I guess this is how it was with us, our bodies drawn together, straining back to a place where we no longer resided, but which was familiar nonetheless, safe; a buffer against impending uncertainty.

Instead of making a right on Lake Shore Drive, which would have taken us to the North Side, to the hospital where Nana had been admitted, my cousin kept straight, heading toward the South Side, where I grew up and where his family still lived. I didn't ask why we weren't going in the direction of the hospital, and, looking back, I think I already knew. But I wanted to make myself believe that I didn't. It was just like the game my sisters and brother and I used to play when we wanted to stretch Christmas. We would wrap up all of our presents again and, the next day, the day after Christmas, pretend as though we were opening them for the first time.

I came up with all sorts of hopeful explanations: Maybe we were going back to my cousin's house to pick up something before heading to the hospital; maybe Mom wanted me to wait there until she was ready for me to come. But every one of these dissipated into the air as we pulled up to the house. I recognized several of my relatives' cars parked along the street out front.

Inside, everyone sat rigidly around my uncle's dining room table. I felt a pinch in my chest as I greeted Auntie, Aunt Rowena, and my other relatives with a kiss. They all managed to contort their faces into smiles which lasted only a few seconds before they fell away. Somebody told me that Mom was on the back porch. I walked through the kitchen toward the open door. My mother's back was turned, wisps of smoke from her cigarette roped around her head. Another cousin, who also stood with her back to the house, turned to look at me as I approached and then looked away, her eyes red and swollen. Mom glanced at me over her shoulder when I stepped onto the porch and reached for my hand. Her eyes were clear, her voice steady as she whispered, "She's gone. She died around three this afternoon."

They had saved this moment for us; my cousins, aunts, and uncle had bit back their tears to clear this quiet space for me and my mother. I cried, unexpectedly, almost involuntarily. I thought that I had made peace with this possibility when Nana first went into the hospital. I thought that I would be relieved. She had been in so much pain for so many years. It had gotten to the point where she couldn't even move around the house. Most of her days were spent sitting in her chair watching television. I knew that she hated that her body could no longer do the things she wanted it to do. For her, this was like a death itself. Last time I visited, she told me how much she was hurting and talked about her funeral, telling me what she wanted and didn't want, as though giving me instructions. I knew she was preparing to leave, and I thought that I was ready to let her go.

Mom pulled me to her, but her embrace felt like she was someplace far from there and had left behind the shell of her body for everybody else's comfort. It seemed wrong, somehow, leaning on her that way; the way we had all leaned on her when Daddy died. I wanted to ask her how she felt. I wanted her to tell me. I wanted to be strong for her. When I tried to hug harder, to pull her closer, she stepped back slightly.

As soon as my voice could break through the steady stream of tears, I asked Mom how she was holding up. "Okay," she said and lit another cigarette. She asked me if I was ready to go inside. I shrugged and nodded yes, smearing the wet traces from my face. We joined the rest of the family at the dining room table.

I sat down next to Aunt Rowena and she covered my hand with hers. I could feel her bones shifting through her palm, the cool metal of her rings. The silence around the table expanded to engulf us, too. It felt as though we had entered a soundproof room where every noise got swallowed up whole, the air pregnant with undigested sound.

It was a silence that I had sensed before, although I had never been inside of it like this, that shrouded the lives of the adults around me with mystery and created a seemingly impassable gulf of secrecy between us; a silence that had kept me wanting and needing more than what was offered. It was this silence that I encountered in the slave narratives, in the loud shouts and protests of the writings from the Civil Rights movement, in my grandmother's house, each time I asked, Who are we? Who am I? What is the meaning of silence? It was a closed window, a veil falling; a train rolling away from a station into the night. It was not remembering and never forgetting. I was born out of this silence and into it. But I was also born into a generation that demanded that everything be explained.

My mother's face shimmered like water. The lights were on. I saw reflections. We had decided to spend the night at my uncle's, neither of us prepared to enter Nana's house without her there. We settled into the same bed, like always, it seemed, although it had been more than ten years since we had stretched alongside each other like this, my body racing to catch hers. I used to crawl into bed next to her, when Daddy worked the night shift, and curl up in the warm spot she left for me when she rolled over to Daddy's side. We used to face one another and whisper in the dark. I would push my leg out all the way and it still wouldn't reach over to her side in my parents' queen-size bed. That night, there was less distance between us, less room to stretch out, and I began to feel the need to guard my space. Our eyes stayed fixed on the ceiling.

"Her leaving . . . I just couldn't touch the thought. I wouldn't let it in." This was how Mom began to recount the day's events, to tell me about Nana's last moments alive and the time they spent together. I noticed the care she took in selecting her words. In my family, we believed in the power of words, the power of the thoughts that inhabited and invested them with meaning. We avoided words like death and dying, sometimes even goodbye, using in their place words like leaving and passing; words open to possibility. For wasn't there always the chance that whatever left would return? And passing was more like an intermittent breeze in summer, backtracking to save you just when you were on the brink of burning.

I watched her as she spoke, and for the first time I felt as though I was really seeing her, seeing through her to the parts she had tried to keep hidden from us. I imagined that she was a lot like me as a little girl. A girl who grew up protected and enclosed in this world of family. She had stability. She could walk down the street and there were always people who knew her. She had routine. Church, family gatherings, dances, parties, groups of friends. But, like me, she was still searching for something. In my case, I always thought it was something outside of myself that I needed—popularity, acceptance, validation. But it was really trying to convince myself that all those good things my family said about me were true, and that I deserved whatever it was that I had.

Mom must've grappled with this, too. Even though she had all of these positive images surrounding her, she was still searching for their reflection, manifestation, within herself. The memories of her childhood that she shared with us seemed to be all good or all bad, more good than bad. This was what she wanted to pass on to her children, some small bit of sweetness for us to carry with us through the trials that we were guaranteed to face in the world beyond our house.

The goodness, the idealism, seemed also a way to shield us from any doubt we may have had about her love for us, doubts which, perhaps, she had growing up. I remembered her telling me that she sometimes felt that her father didn't love her. I had that same ache when I thought about Daddy. I had tried to cut off all emotional ties to him when he died, but I still craved his presence, hungered for his love. Mom and I were still searching for completion, resolution of hunger. Both of us seeking this resolution from men who weren't capable of giving us what we needed. Mom once told me that she wanted a love where she was somebody's center and he would be hers. She wanted someone to take care of her. I used to get so angry at Daddy, even as a young child, because I never perceived him as giving her the love she needed or deserved.

She seemed to project so much of the love she wanted to give and to receive on us, her kids. We became her life. I found myself striving to balance her needs with my own, to have my life and remain connected, for, in many ways, I lived through her, too. I could lose myself in her sometimes; she became my voice, my thoughts. Sometimes, I couldn't tell where her breathing ended and mine began. It was as though we inhabited one body, shared a singular heart.

*I remember her skin, flaccid in moonlight, paler, thicker than mine. I liked the way her knees buckled and were soft like clay. I remember tickling the bottom of her feet, her scratchy heel. These things I knew about my mother. . . . There was a night I dreamed a dream that became surreal in the terror it evoked in me. I was standing beside a grave holding a wreath of red and white flowers. The moment I realized that they were for Mom, was the moment I opened my eyes. I looked over to her side of the bed, but the familiar hill of her body had subsided into wrinkled sheets. I called to her, jumped out of bed to find her. She was in the bathroom brushing her teeth. I told her my dream, and she promised me that she would never leave me. I believed her then, and for many nights afterwards strung that promise around my neck, and it became the asafetida of my dreams . . .*

My mother's face shimmered like water. I saw my reflection blending into hers and turned away.

It was almost like watching a movie, going to the funeral this morning. This is the same thing Mom said about her wedding day. "I felt like I was watching the whole thing on t.v.," she told me once. Sometimes the most monumental events of your life can occur as though they have nothing at all to do with you.

It was such an ordinary day. We woke up early, fought for the bathroom, got dressed. I wore my long black dress and a brightly colored African cloth wrapped around my head. I smiled to think of Nana shaking her head at me. "I'll be glad when you get through with all this Africa mess," she might've scolded. But I figured she and Granny—my grandmother on my father's side, who would be at the services— would rather me wear the wrap than expose the fuzzy twists of my newly forming dreadlocks.

A neighbor had brought over a box of doughnuts, which nobody ate. A black limousine pulled up in front of the house on time. When the driver rang the bell, we rushed toward the door and filed out to the car. It felt like we were going on vacation, rushing to make a flight. Nobody got into the car right away. Instead we stood around bantering over who would sit where, and who would drive, since there wasn't enough room for the nine of us in one car. The driver eyed us impatiently.

As I laughed and joked with the others, the muscles in my face started feeling sore from the smile which had become a permanent fixture since dinner that first night. It seemed that the entire five or six days of planning today had been spent laughing and smiling. Mom, Nicky, and Beth had all gone out and gotten their hair done at an expensive salon. Yesterday we went shopping for new outfits. Today should have been a party.

We settled into the car, our laughter wilting in the stifling severity of the limousine's interior, and finally subsiding into the thickly cushioned seats. But it was only when the driver pulled away from the house that I began to feel my body constricting, folding in on itself. We were really going, leaving the neutral territory my uncle's house had become. Today was no longer an abstraction; laughter, no longer enough to distract us from the tears this day promised.

The night before I had actually considered not going. I didn't think Nana would mind. When we talked about her funeral, she made it clear that she didn't want it to be a big ordeal. I figured I would just stay home and remember her in my own way. The truth was, I was afraid of seeing her, afraid of looking at her body with no life in it. "But the living have to find a way to say goodbye to the dead; you have to grieve. Otherwise there is no closure, there is no going on. This funeral is for us, not Nana." This is what Mom told me when I asked her what she thought about my not attending the services. But I didn't tell her the even larger truth, which is that I was afraid of those tears.

Since I can remember, I have had difficulty crying. I could never stand that moment of opening in a way that felt like slipping, like the ground being yanked from under me; a feeling of weakness when I needed desperately to be strong. Mom cried all the time when we were growing up, and, in the face of her tears, I tried to make myself solid, impenetrable. At school, when the other children teased me, I did everything I could not to cry, for that would've allowed them a glimpse at me on the inside, and the satisfaction of seeing all the damage they had done.

I had become a keeper of tears. But I had also learned that water cannot be kept. Water always seeks to escape. Recently, my eyes had begun to water constantly. My doctor said it was an allergic reaction. I knew it was my body overflowing. Water finds the cracks and crevices and pushes through. Looking out of the limousine's tinted window, I noticed that it had begun to rain. I promised myself to cry.

*Sometimes the house was a womb that gave birth to us again and again.* As we rummaged through Nana's things a few days after the funeral, the stories Nana could never tell me herself about her past began to unfold in my hands. It was always such a mystery to me, not just the facts themselves of Nana's life, but how she and other women in my family organized these facts into lives that were truly their own.

As a young girl, entering my grandmothers' and aunts' houses was like visiting a foreign country and knowing nothing more of the language than how to say, "I'm hungry," or "thank you," or "please." There was an order to their rooms, to their lives, that was completely inconsonant with my own. They ate dinner when it was still light outside and rarely went back for seconds. Their beds were made. There was quiet in their homes. But I was most in awe of their things, all of which inhabited the particular space that they had created for them.

On occasion, after visiting them, I was inspired to organize my own things. In one frenzied afternoon, I put all of my books—three tall bookcases full—in alphabetical order; arranged my one nail polish and the colored lip glosses Mom had just started letting me wear in a neat little semicircle on top of my dresser; and folded all of my clothes. But the meager order I managed to create never lasted. The lip glosses and nail polish would always topple when I closed or opened a dresser drawer. One of my sisters or my brother would take my books and put them back in the wrong place. And then there were things that defied categorization, that refused to be contained in the spaces of my life that I tried to put them in, like my father's drinking, my parent's separation, Daddy's death.

Returning to Nana's house as an adult, I found the dichotomies between my life and the life she made just as apparent. The house was so complete, so full of her, even when she was no longer there. In my apartment in DC, nothing interrupted the whiteness of the walls. Nothing but an echo, running through mostly empty rooms, announced my presence. There was a blank space where my name should have been beneath the bell. My closets were crammed with unpacked boxes. My life felt tenuous. I wanted certainty. I wanted pieces of me to linger in rooms, in hearts, even when I wasn't there. I wanted things to bear my mark. Sifting through these physical remnants of Nana's life, objects I believed she had abandoned long before she died, I was searching for something that would teach me how to feel settled, how to make a home within myself.

*Other times the house seemed empty, even when we were there. And sometimes there was barely enough room to breathe.* The walls bore down and I felt I was a prisoner, choking on memory. Sunlight pressed persistently against our windows and doors. We kept the curtains and blinds drawn. Days became seamless stretches of time, distinguishable only by our closed or open eyes.

When I was five years old, Mom and I made a pact that we would always be friends, no matter what occurred in our lives. I had tested, many times, the limits of our friendship, a friendship as basic as sky, tree, ground. During those days we were each other's best company. Our laughter fell like new snow over the quiet of the house, melting almost as soon as it touched the ground. But it was in continuous supply. We had learned to chat like old ladies, feasting on small details, allowing incidentals to swell until they became larger than the pain neither of us would voice.

Some mornings, when she didn't know that I was awake, I heard Mom's muffled sobs as she cried into the telephone receiver, one of her close friends catching her tears on the other end. At least I hope this is how it was. I hated the thought of her tears evaporating into dead air. Those mornings, I felt us spiraling apart. We were like planets, one revolving around the other, orbits separated by this chasm of silence, of grief, that grew between us. Those tears, tears for her mother, she never cried in front of me. But even if she had, would I have been able to soothe her?

Dear Tasha,

Here, in my mother's house, my home now, I lose myself. I am nobody's little girl. That part of my self-definition was so strong. No matter where I was, I could lean on that knowledge, feel like there was somebody looking out for me, to shelter me, to take care of me when I was sick. I remember the time I had pneumonia and we drove from Boston to Chicago in the dead of winter, just so I could be sick in my mother's house and she could nurse me back to health. She was my touchstone.

I still haven't found the words to say what losing her has meant, how to describe this hollowness. I feel suspended, not ready to move up in the line of women that stretches before us. I'm tired of these perpetual cycles—movement and rest. I want life to stand still. I know you yearn for the same thing. You make these choices, hoping to find a love you can lean on, somewhere to call home, a life that feels like your own. And you just want to stop there. But I have learned that staying in one place, you don't grow, you fade away. You become a stranger to yourself. This letter is to let you know that I'm here. We need to be each other's rest, if only for a little while.

Enough said—for now. To be continued . . .

Love,

Mom

*I had just finished loading my dinner dishes into the dish-washer when Mom called me in DC that evening, about a year ago. She was in Chicago with Nana, who was in the hospital about to undergo surgery on her legs. My youngest sister had been admitted to a hospital in Boston for a kidney infection. My two sisters were by themselves in Boston, a fact which didn't seem to worry them, but which clawed at Mom's heart.*

*For all of our lives, she had tried to make her body into a safety net, a soft place to break and catch our many falls. And with four of us constantly toppling, catapulting, one after another—some-times all at once—off of any number of high and dangerous peaks, places difficult for her to reach, this was no easy task. In my mind, I see an image of my two sisters, my brother, and my-self scattered on top of buildings and mountains, rocky cliffs and treetops, falling. And Mom beneath us, running, holding out her skirt, always making it in time for us to land in its welcoming folds.*

*It would never be Mom's wish for any of us to fall. As much en-ergy as she devotes to catching us, she devotes even more to trying to keep us sturdy, stable, secure in our footing. Still, like any res-cuer, Mom comes alive when the call for help is uttered or sensed, when one of us gets lost in the wilderness of this life or surrenders to danger's pull. But with my sister going into the hospital with-out her, an unthinkable occurrence in our family, Mom felt as though she had let one of us get away; as though she hadn't moved fast enough, should've known not to leave, should've paid more attention . . . should've been there, should've been there.*

*"Should I go home?" I asked feebly. A glimmer of hope ig-nited on Mom's end, as she pondered the possibility. "But then I still have to be in New York by the end of the week," I added, too quickly. Her voice drooped.*

*"No, no. You stay there. It wouldn't make sense for you to travel all the way from DC to Boston for just a day or two. I'll*

*keep you posted. . . . But I may need you to come to Chicago to*
*be with Nana if I have to go home."*
  *"Alright," I agreed, a shiver running through me. "Alright."*

I am the daughter of women rescuers. I have watched
women work their hands into healing. I have seen their skirts
become wind. Redemption hardens the skin around my heel
and on the sole of my foot. Sacrifice thins my blood. I lie
awake nights picturing things not in their places, people
roaming, and worry ways to right them. My heart leaps when
a cry for help unravels in the air. But when it comes to the ac-
tual doing, to calling myself by name, woman, rescuer, I shy
away from duty. I doubt my ability to perform miracles. I lose
faith in magic. I hesitate. I surrender to fear.

I am accustomed to being the one who is saved.


## XIV

I sat among the grown folk, listening to their talk, observ-
ing their ways, wondering about what happened in their
world, which seemed so full of secrets and mystery, a world
to which I, as a child, was denied access. At family gatherings, while my brother, sisters, and cousins ran around the
house, I strategically positioned myself close to my mother,
so that I could hear their conversation without being too ob-
vious.

I loved it when the grown folks gathered and started their
talk. It was a way for me to escape the silence of my own
thoughts. It wasn't even so much what they said, but how
they said it. I loved how they spoke with their whole selves,
using their bodies as much as their voices as they jumped up
from their seats or assaulted the air with their fingers for emphasis, their generous and uninhibited sounds and expres-

sions: snapping a card down on the table with a sharpness that stung just to hear it, raising their voices to sing along with or to comment on a song blasting from the stereo.

Mostly I loved how their language was like a living, breathing thing. Words which could caress and comfort, and which could also hurt the spirit and heart as much as any blow to the body, when they noticed and pointed out your shortcomings. How different their language was from mine, which had been pressed out stiff and flat over the years spent at predominantly white schools; how it seemed to exist in a time and space separate from my own, but which some parts of me understood and longed to know better.

At twenty-three, I was teetering on the edge of that world, old enough, but still confused as to how to enter it; how I would learn to speak the language of grown folks. I wanted to join the movements and music of the adults, add my voice and my stories to their proclamations of life and love. I wanted to know something about the past, something about the lives my family led. But more than this, I wanted to know the secrets that seemed to inform and hold solid the lives I had witnessed growing up.

Since college, I had been reaching back, trying to find some sense of stability; running from the blank walls of my apartment, where most of my things were still packed away in boxes, the book I couldn't write, the love that would not blossom. I was the daughter who had come back home to Chicago, the city where I was born, looking to be born again.

My grandmother and I swung together in silence on the front porch. As the sky turned from the rose shades of twilight to the deep purple of early evening, we looked out over the block. Across the street, Mr. Lane was watering his lawn, while his wife sat almost hidden in the alcove of their front porch. A car pulled up in front of the house next to theirs and its driver honked the horn. The shadowy figure of a teenager slipped soundlessly through a side door and into the front seat of the car, which screeched off into the night.

Sometimes jazz music would drift into the street, when the man two houses down set his speakers out on his windowsill and spun records for the block, providing a soundtrack, sweet and brimming with nostalgia, for balmy evenings. I had watched this scene, these people, from my grandmother's porch for as long as I could remember. They were etched deep in my memory; so deep, it felt as though nothing here ever changed.

"I'm working on this book," I said, easing into the questions I had prepared to ask Nana about her life. "We talked about it a little over the phone the other night before I got here, remember?"

"I remember something about a book. . . . What kind of book did you say it was?"

"It's about the family. Well, not really *about* the family, it's actually more about me . . ." I paused for a breath, trying to figure out how I could explain this thing that I didn't completely understand. "Basically what I'm doing is looking at glimpses of your life and Mom's life to see how they overlap with and impact my own. How the past informs the present. But then I also want to look at the ways my life is different, you know, how things have changed . . ."

Nana nodded silently.

"I wanted to ask you some questions about your life," I said hesitantly. "I want to know how things were as you were growing up and after you got married."

"I don't know what I can tell you," Nana said. "You know, we had some good times. People lived their lives, that's all. Just like you're doing now. Wasn't any different."

Nana was patient with me as I continued to bombard her with questions. What was it like growing up in Louisiana in the 1920s and '30s? How did you meet my grandfather? When did you come to Chicago? What did you do once you got here? But even as we talked about the past, we were both unsure and frustrated, wondering if we were getting through at all to each other. She told me again and again that her life was not special, that she lived and did the things that needed to be done in order to keep living. Yet beneath her responses, I could hear the questions my grandmother asked herself, as she tried to figure out what it was that I wanted from her. *What's all of this about, this going back? What's the point? The past is already gone.*

As I sat talking with her that day, I felt I was running up against a wall with every question. But there was something else that I did not or would not hear. For some time, Nana had been very ill. Several times during our conversation, she would tell me how bad her legs were hurting her, how tired she felt so much of the time, and how she couldn't get out by herself anymore. I remembered Nana as a woman who was constantly going. She would hop on a bus to go shopping downtown, or we would walk the ten or so blocks to the grocery store together without hesitation. My grandmother could clean the entire house by herself and cook holiday dinners for the whole family. It frightened me to see how frustrated she was at no longer being able to do the things she was accustomed to doing for herself and her family.

During the next few days, my grandmother and I began to work together. I helped her complete her chores around the house, things she had put off doing because they were too much work for her alone. We washed the linens, reorganized the pantry shelves, vacuumed the carpet, turned the mattress on her bed, worked in the basement.

Over the years, Nana and I had been getting closer, taking small and timid steps, venturing further into one another's lives. After I started college, our conversations began to stretch beyond the perfunctory remarks and questions about school, grades, and family. We discussed men and friendships, worries, sorrows, everything. I was the one telling the most, but, although she wouldn't say much directly, I also learned a lot about my grandmother through the advice that she gave and in the ways that she comforted me.

During this visit, we picked up where we left off. We began to talk to each other with our hands, with our eyes, as friends. In the evenings, we chatted over dinner about the prison Chicago had become with all the crime that was occurring, about love, loneliness, and hope. I closed my notebook, let go of the questions that I had come to ask, and opened myself up, spread what little of the life I had lived before her for Nana to see, to touch, to criticize, to admire. In turn, Nana showed me a wound that was still fresh and painful, one which she allowed me, in the small ways that I could, to help her nurse.

The day before I left, I watched Nana as she climbed the steps after we had finished our work in the basement. She rested after each step, her breath heavy, her face contorted with pain.

"Go on and start folding those clothes while they're warm," she said to me. "I'm o.k." I didn't move from where I stood at the top of the stairs. The little girl in me was fighting to just drop the clothes and run away.

"You're going to let those clothes get all wrinkled, standing there," Nana admonished again. I stayed where I was.

"What's the point in me folding now when you're just going to come and redo everything," I teased and put the bundle of newly dried clothes on a nearby chair, then walked down to meet her where she was on the stairs. I held out my arm to her. She hedged for a moment and then looped her arm around mine. As we moved on to the next step, I could feel her muscles tighten and was surprised at how strong her grip was. It was this strength, this refusal to stop even in the face of severe pain that had enabled Nana to do the things that needed to be done, as she had told me, to make the best life for herself and for her family that she could.

Nikki Giovanni wrote about the Black Power Movement of the 1960s, "We wanted Freedom to be so much more than paying our bills at the end of the month; seeing our children grow up and go to college. . . . We wanted Magic, and we soured because Freedom is reality."

I was looking for magic, a flash of light, a sign from God that yes, we as a people were struggling and that we would make it through! But I learned from my grandmother that struggle and freedom do not come only in grand and romantic pronouncements, but are as natural as breathing, as ordinary as making sure there are fresh-smelling sheets on the bed, cooking a hot meal, embracing and talking to one another, looking at each other, saying, "good morning," acknowledging one another's presence and significance both in the small world of our home, and in the world surrounding it which often threatened its existence.

The next day, Nana told me how much my help around the house had meant to her. And indeed, she had helped me, too, in a way that I didn't know I could be or needed to be helped. I had come home looking to the past, hoping to find there things that I could use in my life. Instead, Nana taught me something about what it means to struggle, to take the life that you're given and make something. She made me understand that history is not witnessed, but is *made* by human hands, human bodies, working together to survive the circumstances in which they find themselves, and to imagine, to try to create better ones.

Nana taught me that my hands could heal, that my heart could reach out and embrace another, that I had something to give that she, and others who had given me so much, really needed; that history's greatest secret, which is so often overlooked, is that everybody carries history and bears responsibility for that which they create; that the smallest things of life are often its most vital gifts.

She runs her fingers through my hair and smiles, letting me know that they are enough.

*There is a place in the music that opens up for daughters to step inside. A place where women gather, where they strip down to themselves. They are at once the girls they left behind and the women they will become. A place where stories that could not be told in words are reflected in the motion of bodies.*

*Here I learn to dance the dance of daughters, a dance where weaving colorful crêpe paper banners around a maypole becomes the braiding of strands of my stories into those of my mother, my grandmothers, the women before us. Our stories crisscross, one continuing another.*

*I watch the women ease into the rhythm. My movements reflect theirs, faces repeating faces.*

*There is a place inside the music where there is no sound at all, a place where daughters learn to sing, to make peace with contradiction.*

# ACKNOWLEDGMENTS

Thank you with my whole heart and love to:

My mother, Marlene L. Tarpley, for life and inspiration; for incessantly asking, "When are you going to finish the book?" and for reading the entire manuscript—several times—with loving criticism and input that expanded my vision. I couldn't have done it without you.

My grandmother, Anna Mae Dudley, for the valley of wisdom beneath my tongue.

My sisters Nicole and Elizabeth and my brother Omar, for listening, for memories that make me smile.

My great aunts Rowena Crawford and Agnes Lipsey, for stories, for making a space for me in the circle of grown folks.

My grandmother, Gladys Tarpley, aunts Gwendolyn Hilary and Marilyn Lyle. Even though the book focuses on the Dudley side of the family, your spirits and influence were ever-present in my heart as I wrote. Thank you for music and dancing after family dinners, for helping me to find my voice.

Aaron Reed, "the professor," for sharing your wisdom and experience, for your presence in our family.

Mary Cotter, Stefan Griffin, Myronn Hardy, for friendship and laughter.

Professor Len Rubinowitz, for saying "Nothing is too far out of the realm of possibility," for being a bridge between "two worlds."

My editor Deb Chasman, and Tisha Hooks, for giving me the time to write, for having faith that the words would come.

Thank you also to the National Endowment for the Arts and the Massachusetts Cultural Council. Fellowships from each of these organizations provided vital financial support for the writing of this book.